On
Angels'
Wings

MY FLIGHT FROM TRAUMA TO GRACE

GLORIA MASTERS

First published and distributed on Amazon 2021 by Gloria Masters

Auckland, New Zealand.

A catalogue record for this book is available from the National Library of New Zealand

ISBN 978-0-473-54808-7

Cover Design: Ana Marinovic. Top Level Designer, 99 Designs, United States

Photographer: Rachael Tapper, New Zealand

Editor: Isabelle Russell, New Zealand

Proofreader: Brenda Shepherd & Debbie Street

Psychologist: Rachel Grimwood

My Go To: Jackie Kindred

Typesetting: Amy Brown for BookPrint Ltd NZ

Printed and bound by KDP Amazon US

To Jess and Matt,

For your endless unconditional love.

'The only thing necessary for evil to exist is for good people to do nothing.'

Edmund Burke (abridged)

CONTENTS

FOREWORD

Although this book reflects the childhood I had, it is written from my perspective only and others may or may not remember it as I do. Whilst it is an honest account of my experiences, I am conscious that my siblings don't want me talking about what happened and, in fact, never have. Because of this, we have not had a relationship for over twenty years.

I have chosen to write this story at this stage in my life because it is time. Time for me to claim my voice and share my truth. Whilst what is written within these pages is undoubtedly disturbing, my intention is not to shock or bring others down.

My purpose in publishing this memoir is to show not only how I survived, but how I overcame against all odds; how the strength and beauty of the human spirit pushed through to emerge victorious and triumphant.

What you are about to read happened, and it happened to me. From the very beginning, my childhood was one of neglect, abuse and suffering. Because of how I was raised, I could either give in to the daily trauma or find a way to make it to the other side.

I made it to the other side.

NB: All people, places and events referred to in this memoir are real, but in order to protect those I love, some changes have been made, including the omission of one person who is very special to me.

INTRODUCTION

The real catalyst for this book was my participation at a global personal development conference in 2018 alongside two thousand other participants. A pre-requisite for each attendee was to write about four challenging incidents they had experienced during their childhood. As I was recording mine, I had no idea of the impact my words would have and where this would lead.

A few days into the conference, the trainers asked to speak with me. Having read my submission, and after closely observing me, they expressed that they were deeply moved that I in no way appeared to reflect the trauma I had been subjected to as a child and they felt I had something of value to offer the other conference participants. They told me my story would give people hope and a way forward in their own lives and struggles. Their rationale was: if my story were to be heard, it would help people face their own challenges without being burdened by bitterness or resentment. Instead, it would help them to reframe their own lives and experiences through a positive lens. They also felt I had an inner light that shone through with a brightness that could inspire others to shine. I was initially unwilling, as I did not want the attention, nor did I see myself in the way they did.

Eventually, I agreed to talk to my group and afterwards, the penny dropped. The impact was phenomenal. People were deeply moved and inspired, as they lined up to tell me about the challenging situations and experiences that they had suffered through, that, after listening to my story, they now saw somewhat differently. How they could now forgive people in their lives and deal with things they had previously ignored out of fear and shame.

People wanted to touch, hug and thank me. One offered to set up a foundation in my name, while another volunteered to make a movie of my life. I was asked repeatedly to go back to New Zealand and write a book about what had happened to me.

So that is exactly what I did, and here it is.

PROLOGUE

If I just make the loop tighter it will work. Come on, come on, he's going to be home soon. Why won't it go in? I haven't got much time and the buckle won't fit. What am I doing wrong? Why won't it work?

If I just hurried, I would be able to end it all before he came home. I was in the wardrobe, one end of his leather belt hooked around the rail, the other around my neck as I tried to tighten it. But it wasn't working.

No, no, no, my feet are still on the ground. Please, please, just work. But hang on, where would it work? Where could I go that was high enough?

Is that his van coming down the drive? No, no, no.

Run, just run and hide. No, hang on, wait, I'd better put the belt back. Then hide in the wardrobe. Hide, hide, hide.

I had been living with my father for a month when I first attempted suicide.

I was eleven.

BEGINNING

From the time he first raped me, aged four, my father became The Monster. I was born on 24 June 1960, apparently around 5 am. It's too late to ask either of my parents because they wouldn't know. My father is dead, and my mother has no idea. My impression had always been that they were disinterested and angry that I was even born. I knew my mother had wished she wasn't pregnant again. Unfortunately for her, her prayers were not answered.

My name is Gloria, and this is my story.

The earliest photo of me is as a newborn in hospital with one eye open. In hindsight, I have come to realise that this forecast how I would end up journeying through life. I have always seen the world with an awareness and understanding that I can't explain. I just seemed to accept things and manage what happened to me with a kind of knowing.

Most of my childhood I was hungry. I was starved, either to make me look younger for the paedophiles, or as punishment for not smiling and engaging with them enough.

It's therefore no surprise that my earliest memory is one of hunger. I was born into a Catholic family as the youngest of four, where the life cycle was hunger, abuse and neglect.

I remember being a baby, left in a container of some sort in the laundry, crying and crying and crying. No one came, but when someone finally did, it was The Monster. He ejaculated into my open mouth while swearing at me. From that moment on, he became not my father, but my abuser.

FAMILY

Some people should never become parents, my own being a prime example. Neither of them valued the beauty of children and the gifts they bring. Absurdly, they seemed to resent the fact that they were needed to provide guidance and love. Once I was born, they did make sure I was useful, at least. In my father's case, by enabling him to make enormous amounts of money and achieve notoriety in the paedophile underworld; in my mother's, becoming a servant to do her bidding and to reflect her perceived magnificence.

I knew my parents didn't care about me at all, ever. In fact, the most strongly held belief I had about myself was that I was in the way. I don't know why they didn't love me; all I know is they didn't.

My parents were very young when they got married—she was twenty and he was twenty-three. They did what the Catholic Church dictated at the time: found a suitable partner, had the wedding, produced a family and then attempted to manage it all from there.

As the Catholic Church abhorred birth control, the four of us children arrived in quick succession. When I was born, my eldest sister, Christine, was six, my brother, Shane, was four, and my other sister, Debbie, was two. Being the youngest usually meant I would miss out on all the good things going, which were usually few and far between. I wasn't as quick as my older siblings, or big enough to fight for my share. Sometimes, Christine, and more often Debbie, would look out for me, but they were in survival mode themselves.

We lived out in West Auckland, in the suburb of New Lynn, in a basic three-bedroom house with a fourth smaller study. It was considered to be an average house, haphazardly positioned between an industrial belt and a residential area. The local tanning factory was just up the top of the road, and on a windy day you could smell the treated leather from our backyard. At the other end was a large reserve which abutted some fields where horses grazed. The best thing about where we lived was its large quarter-acre section with a creek running through the bottom of it. With large fruit and willow trees on the property, it was a childhood playground of its own. There were many similar houses on the street and lots of growing families living alongside and nearby. Although not a 'flash' house, it was suitable for our family's purposes.

Being able to play with the neighbourhood kids was fun, as I used to love being outside and would only come in when darkness fell, and we could hear the mothers calling their children home for dinner. My siblings and I would return as well, but I never wanted to. Some of my happiest times were had out on that street with those neighbourhood kids, simply because it was safer to be out than in.

To put it bluntly, my siblings and I were all abused —sexually, physically and psychologically. My father, The Monster, took great delight in hurting us and seeing us cry with shame and fear. His abuse was prolific, whether or not my mother was around. Regardless, she knew, and she enabled it. As the youngest, I didn't really understand what was happening, but I remember hearing my sisters cry and begging him to stop. One day, when I was four years old, I rushed in to save Debbie and got a backhander from him that sent me flying across the room where I hit the wardrobe door and crumpled on the floor.

The Monster became so incensed with me that he picked me up by my neck, took me out to the garage and threw me into an apple crate, which he nailed to another one and locked me in. I was warned not to move or speak and that this would be my home until I had learned my lesson. I was terrified. I had no idea where my mother was, but I knew my sisters were inside the house feeling anxious and afraid of what was going on. At first, I cried and tried desperately to make sense of it, as it all happened so fast, but I couldn't. After a while, who knows how long, I realised The Monster was serious and I was there to stay. A small child folded up into two apple boxes defies belief, but somehow deep inside me, I knew I had to survive this.

As the hours passed, I started to panic until something remarkable happened. Out of the corner of my eye, I saw some little Angels playing nearby and they seemed to want to include me in their celestial games. So, I joined in. They were fluttering around, exuding love and inclusion, and I was fascinated. Gentle, soft and full of light, I felt such an affinity with them, I wanted them to stay with me forever. As night was falling, I could hear my mother calling and then my father coming out to break open the box so I could escape. There were no words of kindness or love. Rather, I was roughly dragged up by my arm and pushed onto the concrete floor. When I finally regained feeling in my legs, I scampered off to share my story of the Angels with anyone who would listen. From then on, they were always with me.

There were many such incidents throughout my early years and our home could only be described as dysfunctional and abusive. The outside world had no idea of what went on in our private domain, as these spheres were kept very separate. Unsurprisingly, both of my parents were adept at putting on an act for everyone else.

Slowly but surely, my parents' marriage festered and descended hideously into blame and bitterness. Extreme aggression and dysfunctional behaviour became a normal and expected part of our daily lives. Theirs was not a match made in heaven, rather in hell— certainly for us children. One or the other would be absent for long periods of time to avoid both the other and us. The toxicity of our home environment was ever-worsening, with no love lost between my parents and definitely no love made available for us.

MY MOTHER

By the time I arrived in the world, it was clear my mother was over having children and all of the responsibility that came with it. She was twenty-six, and although she had had three children before me, she seemed ill-equipped to cope. It was fairly obvious that she did not enjoy running a house or caring for us in even the most basic sense, as, apart from being resentful, she seemed to lack the fundamental skills that took. Our house was a testament to that. Dirty washing was always overflowing in the laundry, dishes were piled up and the house was usually messy and smelly.

Back then, mothers tended to be stay-at-home mums, but this didn't seem to fit with her temperament. Being very intelligent and capable meant the mundane trawl through managing a large and unruly family seemed beyond her. At that time, men went to work and came home expecting to be greeted at the door by a warm, loving wife, dinner on the table and well-behaved and bathed children. The polar opposite was true of our household.

To the outside world, we were a normal Catholic family. On the inside, evil lived. I believe that where neglect and abandonment are allowed to thrive, abuse will always find a home. It certainly had pride of place in ours and my childhood reflected that.

It wasn't only my abuse that scared me, it was watching my father abuse my mother as well. The way he would speak to her, frighten her, push her around and degrade her had a deep impact on me. Over time, she took to her bed and largely stayed there. If she wasn't in her room, which was permanently closed off to us, she was off staying at her mother's. We children didn't count, we weren't factored in, rather we were just a nuisance to be sorted out. We were left for so long—alone, unattended, unloved and unwanted—that we became increasingly dysfunctional ourselves. What other option did we have?

I could have accepted it all apart from her neglect and abandonment of me. It was lonely, isolating and soul-destroying. To have my own mother not want me and, even worse, leave me to be abused and mistreated, was unimaginable. Because I had such limited awareness of what was really going on, I had always held the illusion that one day, she would magically start loving and looking after me. Although I hoped, prayed and begged for that to happen, I would come to learn over the years that that day would never come. The only attention I ever got from her was if I demanded it or gave her something she wanted. As a child, I had to get through somehow and I did this by 'reading' what she wanted. To keep myself looked after and cared for meant I had to provide something she required. So that's exactly what I tried to do. But when that didn't work, she was unavailable to me and my siblings were all I had. I had no choice—I needed someone.

Frankly, my sisters didn't need me either, but I was desperate for any attention and love, so I latched on strongly and followed their lead. We schemed little plans to get us more food or to keep us safe. Naturally, as time went on those plans stopped working and we just became more and more neglected and abused.

Although I had no other relationships that offered me any semblance of comfort, I somehow knew that relying on them was wrong and doomed to fail. Debbie was the closest in age to me and so she was the one I tended to spend most of my time with. Right from an early age, I knew she was different. She was sweet-natured, caring and very trusting. I was grateful to her for trying to look out for me, but she could never really protect me from my father or brother, so in the end she just had to give up. I think that broke her heart a little, as she couldn't protect both herself and me. Understandably, she chose herself. That should never have been her responsibility, but it seemed natural given our closeness. Debbie looked out for me and bore that responsibility as proudly and dutifully as she could until it became too much for her and I noticed her withdrawing more and more. She had become a target of my father's abuse because she was too shy to hide from him or leave the house much. I think her soft, introverted nature precluded her from making many neighbourhood friends.

I, on the other hand, would be running wildly through the streets, staying out and away from home for as long as I could, delaying the inevitable. I never wanted to be back there. Even though I was the youngest, I was always the last child in, or at least I tried to be. In the end with Debbie, it became too difficult to coax her out, as her inner world drew her closer in.

My eldest sister, Christine, on the other hand, was bossy and controlling. I could tell she loved me, and she was more like my mother than my actual mother was for two reasons: she was there, and she tried to be kind and helpful to me. I remember her coming into my room to help me get dressed and give me a cuddle. She would often protect me by remonstrating with me about behaving well because my father was in an angry mood. In her own way, she was trying to shield me, but she couldn't win, as if I was naughty, either she would be in trouble or I would be beaten. I think in the end it broke her spirit and she resolved to leave home as soon as she could. She was constantly ordered to do much of our looking after and she became overwhelmed by the level of responsibility left to her. It was shocking and unfair, and I don't know how she coped.

Although initially very loving and kind, over time her scorpion tail would emerge, and she would lash out with anger and fury. Looking back, I see why. It was too much. She was just a child herself, who needed her mum as much as the rest of us. Years later when she was a teenager, she moved out to stay with a nearby aunt.

My brother, Shane, was a bully. He was mean and nasty and took great delight in taunting me and making my life hell, but he got away with it all because he was a boy. He was encouraged to act in this way towards us girls as a result of my mother's disinterest in us and my father's sexist view of gender roles.

I vividly recall being about six years old when Shane left me to drown. We were at the pools which was an unusual treat. I didn't know how to swim, as I had never been taught, and he had offered to take me on his back across the pool. I was so excited, as he paddled out into the depths with me clinging on to him, then, abruptly, he stopped and dumped me. I started to panic as I didn't know how to get back to safety. I struggled to reach the surface but, unable to kick hard enough to keep myself afloat, I started to sink down further and further. I was about to drown. Luckily, a woman with long black hair swam near me, so I grabbed hold of that hair and hung on for dear life. I was pulled to safety, coughing, spluttering and throwing up water.

Even though she unwittingly saved my life that day, she thought I was playing a joke on her. She was understandably furious and let my parents have it. Shane, of course, was nowhere to be seen and denied all knowledge of the incident. He accused me of making it all up. Naturally, he was believed, so I got the hiding for it.

MY FATHER

In my opinion, my father, The Monster, was a psychopath. He was aggressive, perverted and cruel in his behaviour. There was never any empathy or remorse shown towards me and, till the day he died, he never admitted, let alone apologised for, what he did.

As an adult and a father, to behave in the way he did suggests he may have experienced childhood sexual abuse himself. I recall hearing from an expert in this sort of pathology that his mother could have sexually abused him, that he internalised the cycle of abuse and in turn abused his sisters. Although this is conjecture, it would appear to fit the profile and go some way towards explaining the evil acts he committed towards us growing up.

There was a principle that permeated our household—if you had a penis, you had all the power; if not, your job was to serve those that did. I do not recall my mother trying to protect or defend me against The Monster, let alone my brother. Shane's bullying and taunting of me escalated exponentially as I got older. Although I hated him for it, in retrospect he was reflecting the role modelling he witnessed on a daily basis. Keep in mind that although this was going on in our home, it was also the 1960s and the world had begun to change somewhat. It was no longer an entirely accepted norm that all men were superior to women. The Monster, however, did not accept that the old ways were shifting and his sadism reigned supreme.

This was borne out time and time again, as he, and Shane, exclusively wielded the power and control in our household, violently pushing their male superiority onto us while gleefully observing our resulting descent into abject fear and misery. As Shane could do no wrong and was treated like a prince, it was logical that he would even be fed differently to us girls. I'll never forget the day I first noticed this.

I walked into his room and spied oranges on his desk at a time when they were considered a real luxury in our household. I took one, guiltily running to hide somewhere so I could hastily eat it. Since he was a boy, he was also given special food to take to school along with money to spend. This was not a privilege us girls were afforded and usually there was so little food in the house that we learned to steal what we could to feed ourselves out of necessity.

Unfortunately for me, my brother realised someone had stolen one of his oranges, and that day my father gave me one of the worst hidings of my life—not just for stealing, but for daring to even enter my brother's room. This experience was repeated over and over in our home. Plenty of food, warmth, money, treats and fun for him and never any for us girls. What made it even worse was that if one of us was unwell and couldn't eat what was put in front of us, The Monster would scream at us about the 'poor starving children in Africa!' in spite of the blatant hypocrisy of him not just withholding food, but starving us altogether.

Looking back, I grew up thinking that what was happening in our house was normal and that all families behaved the way ours did. But I knew there were secrets to be kept and that I could never ever speak of what happened to me. I knew I would be killed if I did, and so I shut up. The threat of violence was often worse than the violence itself because I never knew when it was coming or how to guard against it. I became hypervigilant and made it my business to know where The Monster was at all times and what mood he was in. I learned how to read him so as to adapt my own behaviour accordingly. Like a chameleon in nature, I was a chameleon at home, becoming skilled at avoiding his insanity, beatings and abuse. I kept as safe as I could by knowing the best way to manage whatever mood he was in. As a child, I didn't always get it right—I was the youngest after all, but I never gave up trying.

Throughout my childhood, The Monster's ever-expanding psychopathic tendencies became harder to satisfy. His initial abuse of us children would never be enough for him, so, over time, the attacks became more sinister and sadistic. In the first few years, though it was just him doing the abusing, the cruel and deliberate methods he used were more frightening than when he started getting other people involved.

A twist to the tale was to emerge, as apart from his 'underworld' mates, I noticed that he was very respectful and considerate around other people. A noticeably different look would appear on his face and he would become quite deferential, calling people 'sir', or giving way to them in a hallway or shop. I found this behaviour strange and confusing, as it was at such odds with his demonic behaviour at home. He seemed able to easily switch this personality on and then switch it off again with equivalent ease. The cleverness of his manipulation of others ensured that no-one ever really saw his true self lurking beneath the momentarily charming surface. It wasn't until years later that I learned that charming and likeable behaviour is ranked among the top traits of psychopaths.

EXTENDED FAMILY

From the time I was a toddler, I was made to spend time with The Monster's extended family. His three sisters, Betty, Olwyn and Iris, were all nice enough, but I loved Aunty Iris the best, as she was so kind and generous. She would openly hug and kiss me, show genuine interest in me and actually seemed to like me. It was her house we would usually go to, as, for some reason, visits to his other siblings were rare. No explanation was given, but I finally worked out why. There was no gain in it for my father. Betty and Olwyn didn't meet the criteria for facilitating child prostitution, whereas Iris and Nana B, his mother, did. My father needed a proper set up including full control of the enterprise, which the others could not provide—Betty, because she didn't seem 'all there', and Olwyn, because she wasn't interested.

There were some occasions when celebrations would be held with The Monster's family. These could include Christmas or adult family birthdays usually held at Nana B's or Iris' homes. At Iris' I could always look forward to plentiful hot meals and sometimes even presents from her. Shortly afterwards though, reality would kick in again. We would be driven home to be greeted by more of the fear and neglect that inhabited our house. I don't know if The Monster's family ever realised quite how vicious and savage he was towards us, as he usually put up a jovial, convivial front around them. He seemed to enjoy spending time celebrating with them, but never even considered that Christmas was actually about children.

I never understood why until recently, but it makes sense that birthdays or Christmas were rarely celebrated in our home. To our father we weren't thought of as his precious children. To him, we were objects, useful for financial gain and professional recognition in the paedophile world. Logically, following that line of reasoning, why would he choose to waste money on an object?

Birthdays were particularly hard in our home. They didn't really exist and even when they were acknowledged, they weren't often celebrated. The one and only time I remember receiving a gift for my birthday was when I was six years old. I opened the bedroom door and sitting outside was a shiny red scooter. I am sure that was the only time I received a present from either of my parents until I was quite a bit older. The gift of the scooter materialised during the first year that The Monster started to make some serious money out of me. Perhaps he was celebrating my special day as he was envisaging a good earning year ahead of him.

Although mainly Auckland-based, we also had extended family in the South Island. I never got to meet them or visit them, but I heard mention of them over the years. In Auckland, however, The Monster's brother-in-law had a house out west which we would be taken to sometimes when my mother was absent or pretending to be sick. On those occasions, we would stay overnight and us kids would be made to wait in a sleep-out on the property. As there was usually quite a gathering, the men would sit outside around the fire and cook meat over it.

One night, what was often unbearable for me became dangerous and life-threatening. As the night drew in, and more beer was drunk, the social gathering escalated into raucousness. Us kids were taken to the back yard and left there until The Monster had agreed on the sexual services we would perform and the corresponding rates. As I was the youngest girl, I was deemed more appealing. I could see the glee on my father's face as he realised how much money he could make from me.

There were logs over and around the fire, and on this particular occasion, my uncle came up with a new and innovative idea. He suggested that the men take turns touching and tickling my naked and exposed body to see how long I could stay balanced while standing on one of these logs. The first one to make me fall off would be the first one to rape me. The bigger challenge was to keep me from falling into the fire. The game proved to be a huge hit and bets were placed on who would win. It only escalated from there, as I was made to balance, stand on one leg and dance repeatedly throughout that long night. As the game continued, the men were encouraged to hit and kick me, pull my hair and attack me to see how long I could stay standing.

Many bets were made, much money changed hands and still I was made to keep going. If I showed signs of fear or of tiring, The Monster would slap me across the face. I was exhausted and crying and fell over so many times. Eventually, when I couldn't move any more, it was over.

I was bleeding, beaten-up, bruised and broken, but this was nothing compared to the shame I felt at being exposed to all of these men laughing at me, taunting me and enjoying my pain and humiliation. Something inside of me died that night and something else was born: hatred towards The Monster.

These nights were to continue over many years and though my extended family continued to be involved in our abuse, Uncle Snow,

Olwyn's husband, was a particularly nasty part of it. I remember seeing him many times and trying anything I could to avoid him. He would openly fondle me in front of family, and I was always made to sit on his knee. Both male and female adults would observe what was going on yet do nothing to stop him. 'Naughty old Uncle Snow,' they would say and laugh at him. Over time, I think what frightened me the most was that not only was I never safe, but I couldn't trust anyone in The Monster's family. As that was where I was required to spend my weekends and occasional evenings during the week, it was an inescapable prison.

For The Monster's family to have been willingly involved in, and even be the instigators of, my abuse, suggests that this was not unfamiliar to them. Oftentimes, those who have experienced intergenerational abuse themselves are more likely to repeat the pattern—similar to my father, I guess. Whilst I have no evidence other than my own anecdotal findings to prove this, my family history seems to support this conclusion.

Throughout my younger years, I grew fonder of Aunty Iris and was always thrilled to go to her place. She was loving towards to me and would encourage The Monster to be less harsh and less physically vicious towards me. She would tell me I was a 'good girl', give me a genuine, warm hug and let me sit with her while she whipped up yummy food. I loved being in her house, learning to bake desserts and cakes. I got to make things for her and loved every minute of it.

Those felt like happy times for me and, as they were few and far between, I relished them. I received something from her I didn't otherwise have in my life: kindness. The dream, however, would come crashing down to earth as, unbeknownst to me, there was an agenda at play. Aunty Iris was grooming me. She was nominated as one of two family members to hone and perfect my childhood prostitution skills. Once I realised what was really happening, it was much too late. There was nothing I could do. I had no power, and no one would listen to me anyway. Although she remained kind and gentle towards me, she was determined in her task and so the haven I had felt her place to be, was quickly replaced by yet another place of misery.

Over time, one of the worst things about being in her home in Devonport was that she had an adult son, David, living with her. He, too, sexually assaulted me at will and was in fact encouraged by Aunty Iris to be the guinea pig while I practised my sexual techniques on him! He seemed to enjoy this and would take full advantage of the opportunity. Of course, the older I became, the more I realised that hell was here on earth, I didn't need to die to go there. It was all around me and inhabited my world. My sole mission was to try and survive while hoping there would be some respite soon. It just never felt as if it was going to happen. David had an awesome black leather jacket and occasionally he would let me touch it. It was heavy and smelt of leather and oil, reminding me of a movie I had watched. I never really noticed the insignia on the back; it didn't seem important to look, I just wanted to try it on and pretend it was mine.

I also admired David's impressive motorbike—the sound, the look and how cool it all seemed. I would repeatedly ask to go for a ride on it, becoming quite a nuisance, until the day I realised he was part of the gang I would eventually be leased out to. It was at that moment I realised my life was on a dangerous path, one I had no control over.

Nana B also welcomed me into her home with open arms, mainly because I had the potential to be a top earner, but as a small child I didn't understand any of that. All I knew was that I was allowed to play inside, that people living there didn't hate me and that I could usually eat whenever I wanted.

Nana B adored The Monster. She used to wait on him as if he were a king. It didn't seem at all unusual to me that he bossed her around. After all, he was in charge of everything else in my world.

Hers was a place I initially liked going to. She was kind, her house was warm, and she gave me money to buy lollies at the shop. Having been so deprived of these 'luxuries' in my own home, I thought I had died and gone to heaven. I didn't see the manipulation behind the grandmotherly gestures, I didn't see that she was just another adult grooming me, I was just so relieved to be warm and fed.

An ongoing pattern began to emerge. When my mother's prolonged absences occurred, The Monster would be left to care for us, so the logical step was for Nana B to take over. She would either come to our house or, being the youngest, I would be sent to hers. In retrospect, it suited The Monster's purposes perfectly as although Aunty Iris was charged with training me, it was Nana B that initially taught me the fine art of prostitution.

I was six years old.

Nana B's house was in Kingsland and it was from her front bedroom that I was hired out to various men over the years. They would arrive in flash-looking cars wearing dark-coloured suits. I was told they were very important and that I had to be nice to them and do everything they asked me to. If I was good, there would be treats for me later. Usually, two or three men would be there at the same time. They would take turns waiting in the front parlour with Nana B or The Monster until it was their time with me. I was initially excited about the ice cream I was promised later, or the other treats I would sometimes be given. Inevitably though, I was hit by the realisation of what was actually happening to me and it was at that point that I dissociated.

Dissociation is where you leave your body and go somewhere else in your mind. As a young child, one of my favourite places to travel was a field of daisies where a white winged horse would appear and whisk me away. I loved that horse and never wanted to stop riding it. We explored the universe together on magical journeys. Naturally though, I would always return to my body, jolted from my daydream as confusion and fear swept over me. A man's face would loom in my mind with a clarity and focus I couldn't vanquish no matter how hard I tried. Not all of the men were nasty and violent though and while most paedophiles are, by their very definition, monsters that prey on defenceless and vulnerable children, a few would show kindness towards me and it was those gentler beings with whom I felt the safest. Not at home, not with either parent, but with a soft-natured paedophile.

As I grew older, school holidays and weekends tended to be when The Monster would take me to Nana B's home to supposedly 'give my mother a break'. Although I hated what I had to do there, I remember fleeting moments of happiness during these times because I was sometimes given bigger treats once all the men had left.

Between the ages of about six and nine, my prostitution repertoire developed, as Nana B showed me how to be more alluring, how to move and contort my body and how to flirt successfully with the men. I really became quite skilled at seduction. In fact, as it was often the only positive attention I received from the adults around me, I enjoyed the acknowledgement. The shame and guilt I felt later in life were soul-destroying, but I was so starved of anything resembling kindness or love, that I clung hopefully to positive words from anyone who would give them.

My personality was always a bit cheeky, which seemed to appeal to the men who paid for my services. Sometimes they would give me money in addition to what they had paid The Monster or Nana B, but if either found out, I would be locked in Nana B's downstairs shed for a day or two. When that wasn't enough to punish me, a large and scary dog would be put in there with me. Quite quickly, I learned to give them any money the abusers gave me.

The Monster and his mother were constantly looking for ways to squeeze more money out of leasing me, and using dogs became an obvious choice. One of the more sadistic ways they did this was to chain me up naked and put meat on my genitals. On command, the dogs were released to rip the meat off me. I was almost catatonic with fear and The Monster, being the astute entrepreneur he was, saw the value in exploiting it. Within a month, that was added to the list of services I would provide. Apparently, men would pay to watch that and from there it was only a step further to bestiality.

I started having seizures during those times and it was at that point The Monster began investigating how to seriously drug me so I would be more uninhibited and not so frightened. The drugs were used for the customers' benefit, not for mine. If I was too frightened, I couldn't perform well. The rationale being that no one wanted to waste good money on a terrified and traumatised child.

On my mother's side of the family, her siblings were all girls, Cathy, Barbara and Margaret and, with the exception of Margaret, they were all married. Interestingly, my mother chose to see things differently when it came to my behaviour around the men in her family. Because my conditioning had been to please men sexually, I thought it was natural. So, it came as somewhat of a shock as I realised that not all men wanted to hurt and use me. My grandfather and uncles were not paedophiles and were therefore not interested in abusing me sexually. Ignoring and tolerating me were the best they had to offer, and I could cope with that easily. But what I hadn't been able to process was that I was safe in their homes—truly safe. When I finally did realise, it became a night I never forgot.

I was nine years old and staying with Mum's sister and her husband to give her yet another break. I had a great time, was given an Enid Blyton book to read and had a hot fresh bath all to myself! What a treat, as in our home baths were a Saturday night event and being the last one in meant cold, dirty water. To have one run just for me was heaven. I decided then and there that I never wanted to leave their house, ever. I was served nice hot food and I started to help around the house, anticipating their needs and fulfilling them. You see, I thought if I was quiet and respectful and did nothing to draw attention to myself, they might let me live with them. Wouldn't that be something?

During that week, I came up with an even better way to convey my gratitude. I tried to 'please' my uncle by touching his penis through his trouser leg and kneeling down to perform oral sex. He leapt up out of the chair, called my aunty into the room and started yelling at me for touching him inappropriately and told me to get out. I didn't understand why he was so angry. Everywhere else I went this was expected and demanded of me and here I was giving it to him for free. I thought he would be delighted. My aunty was disgusted and asked me what was wrong with me that I would behave like that. She then called my mother and told her to come and get me. My mother was furious, mainly because she had to drive from her mother's house to pick me up and drop me back to The Monster. I had ruined her night and her only choice, or so she said, was to drop me back home and then leave again. That was to become the ongoing pattern with her, leaving me with him.

On the drive home, she told me I had ruined her life. She yelled at me all the way and told me I was a bad, naughty, dirty little girl and would never be allowed near that particular uncle ever again.

Looking back, it seems impossible that, once again, no one thought to wonder why a little girl would even think to do that or wonder why she assumed it was the way she should show gratitude. Rather, they decided I was a wicked and bad child who should be punished. And so, punished I was. When The Monster was told about it, he took off his belt and laid into me, but I know it wasn't because I came onto my uncle—it was because I tried to give it away for free.

My maternal grandparents were not friendly or warm towards me. I wasn't all that welcome in their home. I recall the words 'ruffian', 'disgusting' and 'smelly' being thrown out to describe me. I was usually ignored and treated with thinly veiled disgust. Partly because I was naughty and partly, I suspect, because that's how my own mother saw me.

I was 'allowed' to play outside, but that was it. When it came time to kiss Nana goodbye, she would emphatically turn her face away so that I could only graze her cheek. Her intolerance and distaste towards me were obvious as she never liked, let alone loved me. I guess I shouldn't have been surprised, as it was, after all, becoming a feature of my life. The only time adults showed interest in me was if I could please them in some way.

Twice I was sent to stay with my maternal grandmother over the school holidays, and I vividly recall how uncomfortable it felt. I was always expected to fit in, be quiet and not demand anything of her, in other words behave like an adult. It was austere, unforgiving and lonely. I never ever felt comfortable with her, and the feeling seemed to be mutual.

Although my mother had told me that Nana loved me, I knew it was a lie. It confirmed for me that adults often disregard children and their instincts. Children know when they are loved, and they can tell when words don't mean what they say. My mother used to tell me that her mother was very wise and loving and kind. I never saw that in her at all, as a small child, as a teenager or as an adult. Maybe my mother was trying to convince herself—who knows?

BREAKUP

Although the night my parents ended their marriage came as a surprise to my siblings and I, the magnitude of it would not hit until months later. When they told us, I was already so conditioned to the ongoing trauma and abuse that underlined my existence, I could only respond from survival mode. The significance of that night was lost on me in that moment.

Being as detached and selfish as my parents were, their marriage break-up was delivered to us in the most traumatic way possible. We were all ordered to come into the lounge, stand in front of them and form a line. We were told to be quiet and listen very carefully. They explained to us that they were separating and going to live apart, and that my mother would be the one leaving. Our job was to choose which parent we wanted to live with: stay with our father or leave the next day with our mother. Stunned silence filled the room, all of us too shocked and scared to speak. It was then made very clear that once the decision was made, there would be no going back, and we would have to live with the consequences of our actions. Finally, we were told we had to decide right then and there.

As I watched my sisters' reactions, I observed my father doing everything he could to get them to stay, even bribing them with treats and experiences that would never eventuate. They said no. When my turn came, he offered me a hairbrush of my own, which I admit was tempting. I could see it in my mind's eye: a pink one with a matching comb and mirror set sitting on my dressing table. The height of luxury, I would be so cool. I could see myself brushing my hair and flicking it to one side, then checking in the mirror to see how it looked. Yes, I thought, I could do that. But then I looked at my mother and wondered who was going to look after her if I wasn't there? You see, that role in her life had become mine.

As the seconds passed, my dilemma only grew. I really wanted that hairbrush set. I'd seen it in Woolworths and loved it. My father noticed that I was wavering, so he threw in a horse. Well, as an avid horse lover, that clinched the deal. I could see it now, riding around the paddocks on my pony, with everyone wanting to be my friend and thinking I was so lucky. It was as simple as it sounds. I fell for it and consequently chose to live with him. I turned to look at my mother with guilt and shame in my eyes, seeking her forgiveness and already berating myself for letting her down so badly. Our eyes met, but the only thing I saw on her face was sheer blind relief that I had not chosen her.

To say this was one of the most significant events in my life is understating it. I should never have been made to choose. It was wrong on so many levels, little did I know this one decision was to prove not only devastating but also extremely dangerous for me. The unspoken pressure they put on us to decide our future, the way we were made to line up to choose which parent we wanted to live with and the complete lack of interest my mother had in protecting me against my father were all overwhelming for me. The magnitude of that night would be revealed over the next eighteen months, but no one could have anticipated the enormous consequences it would have, let alone me.

Unsurprisingly, Shane chose to remain living with my father—why wouldn't he? All of his needs were quickly met; he was the 'golden child' after all. I was left with a loop in my head questioning why my mother didn't want me living with her, or at least why she didn't try to put up any kind of fight for me. Perhaps it was to do with money or the size of the house she was moving into, or maybe she was just overwhelmed. Whatever the reason, her relief was crystal clear and so I picked it up and carried the weight of it until it became too heavy for me to bear. I was also feeling confused as to why she left my father, and it was not until decades later that she finally admitted she couldn't tolerate any more of his physical, mental and emotional abuse towards her. As her words sunk in, I realised that at the time of the breakup, she was thirty-eight and I was only eleven. If she couldn't cope any longer to the point of fleeing, in what parallel universe would she imagine I could?

I don't know how disappointed The Monster was by the marriage ending, as by then he had already been living his own life for many years. I do think he felt embarrassed and his pride was hurt. As a psychopath, he couldn't possibly tolerate that without extreme emotions surfacing and ultimately strong retribution being taken. Unfortunately, it was me who bore the full brunt of it, as once my mother had fled with my other siblings, I was the only female left. It never seemed to register with him that I was only a child, or if it did, he didn't care.

Up until that point, our home had been increasingly unhappy and unsafe. From then on, it became deliberately cruel and menacing with evil lurking in all corners.

The agreed access rights allowed me to visit my mother every second weekend and half of the school holidays. For my sisters, it was different. They were older than me and for some reason could choose whether they saw my father or not. Debbie was thirteen when they separated and had been attending boarding school for a few months. She been placed there because she was really struggling to cope at home. Uncharacteristically, my mother was concerned enough by Debbie's behaviour and declining mental health that she took action and chose to send her away from home. I was happy for my beloved sister but devastated for myself. This was partly because Christine, who was seventeen by then, had also been granted permission to live and work away from home. She had been safely living with my aunty in Glen Eden for some months. It took me a while to work out why I was so distraught but when I did the realisation threatened to break me with its starkness: I was now the only girl left available to my father seven days a week.

Before the breakup, Debbie's choice was sometimes to remain at school over weekends. She would always come home during holidays though, and Christine would call in regularly as well. After the breakup, however, neither ever willingly spent time with my father or came to the house. This meant I hardly saw them. Shane, on the other hand, rarely, if ever, chose to visit my mother and for some reason this was deemed acceptable by both of our parents.

The day my mother and sisters left was, in my father's view, a cause for celebration. He declared that we would do this by having fish and chips for dinner and lemonade to drink. The only other times in my life I had lemonade were at the occasional Christmas or birthday party. As my father raised his beer, he told us that from then on, we were to refer to my mother as 'the fat bitch'. I felt a bit worried about that, but laughed along with him and Shane, knowing it was better to do that than to speak up. He was nice to me and seemed happy I had chosen him. He said how I had always been the favourite girl and how the others were useless. He told me that as I was the smart one, he would look after me and 'show them' just what a big mistake they had made by choosing their 'fat useless mother'. He then paraded around the kitchen, imitating my mother and making me imitate my sisters. It was scary, but he was smiling, so I did what he asked. It broke my heart a little bit, that betrayal of my sisters—I had to keep him happy though, as I knew going against anything he said or did could be hazardous for me.

He went on to explain the rules of the house now that 'the fat bitch' had gone. Basically, he said I had been chosen to do 'everything' for him and Shane and that meant running the house for them. I didn't really understand what he meant—that would come later—but I was smart enough to act pleased with this arrangement.

After dinner, I was feeling quite chuffed with myself. I had a full tummy, I was getting my own horse and life was about to change for the better. I went to sleep dreaming of horses, even hearing the *clip-clop* of imaginary hooves, when I woke to realise there was actually a clattering noise coming from the kitchen. I sat up, heart pounding, suddenly feeling very afraid. The next thing I knew, my bedroom door was flung open and I could see The Monster holding something long and shiny. As I adjusted to the dark, I could see it was a knife. He dragged me out of bed by my hair along the carpet to his room. He was screaming at me because my mother and sisters had left him. He held the knife to my throat and demanded to know what they had said and why they had left him. I was struggling to breathe and crying so hard I couldn't form the words, but even if I could, I would never tell him the truth. If he knew for one minute that they hated him and feared him, he would kill me. I couldn't risk that. He kept kicking me and screaming at me, 'Tell me, tell me, tell me!' I eventually said I didn't know and that they probably felt bad about it. That seemed to mollify him for a moment, then he pulled me upright, pressed the knife up to my face and yelled, 'If you ever leave me, I will find you and gut you like a pig.' He then proceeded to hit me, rape me and throw me onto the floor. He went to bed and left me lying there.

That night signified the beginning of my new existence under The Monster's care. I had considered life until then to be hard, comprised of stealing food to eat or doing my best to become invisible to avoid the beatings and rape. What I would come to realise was that 'before the breakup' I was relatively safe, compared with 'after the breakup' when I would *never* feel safe again. Daily humiliation and degradation were now piled onto me, as I was subjected to horror beyond imagination at the hands of a deranged psychopath. I still find it remarkable that I was able to find a single aspect of my existence to keep me going and I credit this to my Angels.

Whether it was the light outside my room, or the shadows cast on the wall, I would at times feel a presence around me. Whatever it was, or however it presented itself, I knew there was something deep inside of me calling me to survive, I just didn't know what it was. What I do know is that I trusted it, spoke to it and felt seen and heard.

Being so young, I had not taken into account how desperately I would mourn my sisters and how much of a loss their leaving would be. I missed them terribly. I hadn't realised the emptiness their absence would create—they were my rock and though not yet adults themselves, they were more protective of me than my own mother. I trusted them, and now there was a gaping hole where their love and care had once been. I now had no one left with whom I felt safe. The sense of isolation would grow over time, as I became more depressed and anxious. I was trapped forever, or so it felt. Why they were given the freedom to choose and escape seeing him at all felt unfair and wrong to me. I couldn't understand it. It felt like my mother used me to keep my father happy, that I was the sacrificial lamb for her, as at least if he had me, she could feel better about leaving. She did not or chose not to notice, that I was at serious risk of losing my life and/or sanity. I was her baby, her youngest child, the one who needed her love and protection the most.

It seemed that once I had made my choice to stay with my father, I was rejected and scorned by both sides: in my father's house and in my mothers. I didn't fit anywhere—it was as if I didn't exist. Although my sisters may have felt pity and compassion towards me, they were safe. I was just a reminder of what they had escaped from and they certainly did not want to remember. Unconsciously, they began reflecting my mother's attitude towards me, making me the 'bad one', and the representation of all their abuse and suffering. It was unfair and, once again, isolating and devastating for me.

The prison I was in had many jailors, all of whom were related to me.

Whenever I had access to my mother, I tried to show her how bad it was for me, but she wasn't interested. She would ignore me and eventually tell me to 'just be quiet' or 'go away'. As it became more obvious that she wasn't going to keep me safe from harm, I realised it was up to me. I had to find a way to keep myself as safe as possible.

Back at my father's home, I decided to be as observant as I could and did some childlike research. This culminated in a little strategy I hoped would work. I had noticed that he was always nicer to me if I was smiling and appeared happy to be his slave. He also loved it when it looked like I 'enjoyed' the deviant sexual attacks and rape. So, as my only options were magnifying this behaviour or sinking into the black hole of depression, I decided to always be compliant and happy in my outward appearance, whilst showing my 'gladness' at being sexually abused. I noticed it started working, not always but more often than not, and that is what gave me the sense of strength and courage to keep going. Perhaps if I could get through this one day at a time, I might just live to tell the tale.

To this day, I don't know how I knew to do that, but I think somehow my Angels were involved. As what I learned to do to survive is considered self-preservation and can only come from having a 'sense of self', it is usually nowhere to be seen in a person as young and traumatised as I was, but somehow, it was alive and well in me.

Although behaving in this way made me physically ill and I hated him more every day, I felt I had no choice. It was becoming more apparent that his psychopathy knew no limits or levels and it wouldn't be long before either he, or I, would descend into madness. There was something innate within me that knew I could not let it be me, that I needed to survive, that I had to keep the light that was me alive. It was so strong in me, it was almost as though my Angels were determined to keep me going and I just had to figure out how.

Over time, I worked out my biggest challenge was outwitting and outlasting his depravity, which I did without him knowing what I knew:

that he enjoyed inflicting as much humiliation and pain as he could. My survival strategies grew to accommodate this, almost anticipating his every move and adopting a 'false self'. The only problem being I started identifying more with that than who I actually was. That ultimately scared me more than anything else and become a significant challenge for me as an adult, for if I wasn't that false self, then who was I?

My other major challenge every second weekend was finding a way to integrate myself back into my mother's and sisters' lives. I felt alone, unwanted and disliked. I was suffering hugely, but no one would help me. To survive, I needed to find a way to get some positive feedback or attention. I adopted what children in dysfunctional families do: I assumed a role that would get me noticed and fervently hoped it would hold some appeal for my mother. This role would not only need to help me survive in rejecting and neglectful conditions but also allow me to adjust to the ever-changing landscape around me.

I chose to be 'the carer', both instinctively and for reasons I was conscious of, I naturally fit 'the carer' mould and realised I had been doing it automatically for years. I slotted into this role very easily, as I had a kind nature and natural empathy for others. I had also noticed over time that if I was able to provide my mother things before she needed them, she was nicer to me and occasionally gave me some attention. Sometimes she even told me I was a good girl, and that alone was enough to keep me going for the fourteen days between access visits.

It was during those visits that I would mainly sleep 'the sleep of safe exhaustion', or cling to her. I remember I would beg her not to take me back to him, even hiding under the house so she couldn't find me. However, she always managed to, and I would be taken back to him. She would not stand up for me or defend me in any way. It was obvious she didn't want me with her. When, as an adult, I challenged her on this, she always said, 'You chose to stay with him.' My standard behaviour was to follow her around like a puppy and stand as close to her as I could. She grew annoyed with me, didn't understand it and would constantly try and get me to leave her alone. But I couldn't. She was always pushing me off onto the other girls, who didn't want me either. Why would they? They were probably starved for attention as well. Naturally, my mother never asked why I was so clingy, or what was wrong with me. Not once did she ever seem interested in what was happening at home.

In later years, my mother stated that she had no idea of what had been happening to me throughout my childhood. The reality was that I tried to tell her many times, but she refused to hear it. Whenever I would start, she would either change the subject or ignore me. In every way I could, I showed her how traumatised I was. Now, looking back, it is obvious that by ignoring me she kept the secret hidden and buried it deeper because it suited her. I know I cried and clung to her those initial Friday nights till she drove me home Sunday afternoons, begging, pleading and negotiating with her not to take me back. I would do anything for her, anything if she would just not take me back there. Her stock-standard reply was, 'The Judge has ordered this and we have to do what he says.' The truth of the matter was that she didn't want me and was relieved when I would leave for another fourteen days. I realised, in the end, that I was just in the way and something to be tolerated. She never saw me as a person, she saw me as a function. I was 'something' not 'someone'. It is astounding to now realise that both of my parents could only see me as an object rather than the child I actually was.

My mother and I fell into a pattern: as soon as her weekends were up, I was inevitably taken back to hell. My confusion, fear and anxiety all threatened to overwhelm me, as well as the arduous task of finding the resilience and courage I so desperately needed to return to The Monster and his 'everyday life'. The resoluteness with which she would take me back was almost as cruel as The Monster's treatment of me. His behaviour was always overt. Hers was covert and sneaky. She never bothered checking as to why I was so miserable at having to leave her side, but she would have needed to be blind, deaf and dumb not to see my depression and suffering. I soon realised I only had myself, so I retreated inwards for internal guidance. The strength I had to find, the resources I had to utilise and the smile I had to fake, all ended up coming from within and beyond me. My Angels stood by me and carried me through. They saw all the horror I suffered, the relentless fear I felt, the transition I had to regularly make, and the complete denial from the only person who could have saved me—my mother. Realistically, I had no one living who cared, and had those Angels of mine not surrounded me with love, I know I would have given up.

HORROR

The reality of life without my mother hit and darkness began to shroud everything around me. The light had always been my go-to, but I was finding it harder and harder to see or sense it. It all began to feel like too much. I was overwhelmed with fear at home and sick with her loss. At least when she had been in the house, The Monster's behaviour was somewhat tempered, unlike now where there were no boundaries. He did whatever he liked, whenever and however he liked. He encouraged my brother to join in, and any form of abuse was a given, but once night drew in, it would inevitably become several shades darker.

I was always the target, always the victim, always the scapegoat, always the bad, wrong, weird and ugly one. I was beaten, punched and kicked, as well as spat, urinated, shat and ejaculated on. I was tied up, whipped, starved, ridiculed, taunted, teased and manipulated. I was always scared and didn't know how to get help. No one seemed to be interested and there were no safe adults I could turn to. Slowly but surely, the realisation dawned on me—there was no way out. I really didn't want to live anymore, and I didn't know what to do.

Safety meant various things to me during that time and changed daily. I thought I was safe if I didn't hear The Monster's footsteps down the hallway, or if he drove off somewhere. Eventually, I learned how foolish I was to trust his absence, as it usually transpired that he had something more sinister in mind.

There was never any escape for me and though I made various attempts to run away, I was always caught and brought back home. One day, The Monster took it a step further. He was apparently humiliated that I had hidden in someone's car and been discovered at their home the next day. When I was returned to him, he laughed with them, talked about their next catch up, then waved them off. Once the door closed, he punched me in the face, threw me to the ground, sodomised me and then kicked me several times. Later, when it was dark, he came storming down to my room, dragged me down the hallway by my hair and threw me into the car. He threatened, 'You are going to die today.' I shrank back into the seat, shaking uncontrollably.

This became a common ploy with him, he would often use death threats to either stop me from ever speaking out or to punish me in some way. He threatened that if I ever did tell anyone, he would kill not only me but my sisters as well. Although he was to repeat this many times over my life, I always believed him. By then, I knew what he was capable of. Usually, his threats would be the result of some imagined misdemeanour I had committed, and part of me was hopeful that this time the punishment would at least be bearable.

As we drove along the road, he stopped the car, violently pulled me in the front with him, opened the car door and pushed my head down outside it. He then instructed me to stay there and started driving the car whilst threatening to drop me. This went on for several minutes that felt like hours, and the absolute terror I felt was indescribable. I could feel the wind on my face as well as the heat coming up off the asphalt and I was sure I would be thrown out of the car. Eventually, when he had had enough, he pulled me up by my hair, threw me into the passenger seat and drove me home. I was too scared to sleep that night, the images of the road rushing up to meet me playing over and over in my mind as I relived every terrifying second.

A few days later when he was out, I waited until just on dark when there was a lot of traffic passing by. I stood outside the house until a big van came towards me. At the last moment, I stepped out in front of it. The driver managed to swerve just in time to miss me. He parked the van, came up to me, furious and asked what I thought I was doing. The squeal of his brakes had attracted my neighbour's attention and she rushed over to see if I was okay. She took me over to her house, gave me a sweet cup of tea and a biscuit and made me stay with her until The Monster arrived home. She took me over to him and explained what had happened. He smiled and was most profuse in his gratitude and fake concern for me. Once the front door closed behind him, he was incandescent with rage and told me that if I wanted to die, he would be the one to do it.

He waited till it was very late, woke me up and told me to lie in the driveway. He then walked to the van, started it up and began driving towards me. I thought he was going to run me over, as the van came closer and closer until the engine was right above me. The Monster sat there and started calling out, 'It's your fault, it's you that's making me to do this, why are you so fucking bad? You're just a worthless bitch. If you weren't like this, I wouldn't have to do this to you.' He then reversed backwards and forwards over and over again. I urinated in fear and cried uncontrollably, which triggered hysterical laughter in him, and he asked, 'Any last words, filthy bitch?' Time stood still as I endured this horror. When he finally turned the engine off, my punishment was to lie in the driveway for the rest of the night.

The next morning, The Monster came outside and seemed shocked to find me there. He asked, 'What the fuck do you think you're doing out there?' He then demanded that I 'stop making a show' of myself. He had clearly forgotten what he had done. I was trembling with cold and so traumatised that I couldn't even speak with how much my lips quivered.

That day after school, I climbed into bed and started crying and begging my Angels, God, anyone who was listening, for help. I just couldn't see a way out and couldn't take much more. Rain was spattering against the window and I must have fallen asleep because when I woke, the sun was shining, reflecting light onto my wardrobe door. Its shimmering glow made me feel less alone. Comforted, I got up and started cooking dinner.

Back in those days, being eleven meant plaiting your hair and chewing bubble gum. I wasn't particularly sophisticated or savvy, I was just a scared, traumatised eleven-year-old child, desperate to find an escape from the misery that trapped me. Finding none, I sank further into depression. I took to lying in bed most days, only getting up if I had to. I was lying under the covers one day, staring at the wall, when he walked in and demanded, 'What's wrong with you?' I said I was missing Mum. He told me to pull myself together and that there was nothing about her to miss.

It was during this period that my father increased involvement of other more sinister, groups into the dark world we inhabited. He already had many underworld contacts throughout Auckland, but he was about to up the ante by having me perform for these new associates: the gang he had connections to, a K Road (Karangahape

Road in Central Auckland) nightclub that my father began leasing me out of, as well as the gentlemen's club he was a member of. The abuse became so prolific, I never knew at what point I would be ripped out of my bed, thrown into the van and driven to some unknown destination so my father could rent me out and earn big money. I was grateful for the drugs he would give me with increasing regularity, as my night shifts and weekend workload became ever more demanding. Feeling out of it, drifting in a mind-altered haze, was better than feeling frightened and enduring each experience with searing clarity. The drugs of my father's choice back then were cannabis, heroin and a cocktail of others, which he would have no qualms forcing on me. His increasing descent into destruction made his behaviour more depraved and out of control, and as a result I found it ever more intolerable and harder to survive.

If I hadn't had a connection with my Angels, I don't think I would have survived this time in my life. Seeing them kept me going through the darkness that engulfed me. Where such strong evil exists, having a close presence around me helped. It kept me resilient, and resilience was all I had.

Being resourceful by nature, I worked out that if I wasn't at home, my father couldn't hurt me, so I did everything I could to avoid being there. I would either stay at school as long as possible or walk the neighbourhood right up until it got dark. It was dangerous for me to go home, so I would either clean up the classroom, pick up rubbish or hide in the toilets. Every day, one of the nuns would tell me to go home. If I remained at school well past the final bell, they would always find me, aware that I was somewhere on the school grounds. Although they must have wondered, they never asked me why I didn't want to leave. I was a child clearly signalling I didn't have a safe home to go back to, yet had they, or anyone, asked me what was going on, I don't know if I could have answered them anyway. My behaviour at school was always attention-seeking and if that meant being strapped by the nuns for being naughty, I didn't care.

I just wanted someone to notice and to help me. I didn't have the words to explain the way I was feeling, the situation I was trapped within. My eleven-year-old self could only express through other ways that things were terribly wrong and I was very unsafe.

It was a few months later when I noticed my tummy was getting larger. I couldn't understand why I would be gaining weight, as I wasn't eating that much, and The Monster made sure I stayed underweight and skinny enough so that my bones protruded. I tried to hide it as best I could and then realised that my period hadn't come lately. Because I was so young, I didn't really know what that absence meant, but it didn't take long for The Monster to realise I was pregnant. He flew into a rage, told me to get my stuff and took me to his mother's house. She took me into her room, undressed me, checked me out and told me I was definitely pregnant. When she went out to my father and told him, he screamed at me for being a 'stupid slut'. Together, they decided the only option was for me to have an abortion. But who could do it? I'd never heard of an abortion before, so I wasn't sure what it meant. Whatever it was, I just knew it couldn't be good.

After a prolonged discussion, with potential names thrown around as to who could undertake the procedure, they decided Nana B would be the one to do it. I was made to stay the night while she planned the technique she would use and the equipment she would need. The next day, she gave me something to drink. I don't know what it was, but it tasted strange and my tongue thickened in my mouth until I couldn't speak properly. Dizziness swept over me. As a woozy sensation set in, Nana told me not to worry. It was quite normal, she said, and it would all be over soon. She got me to lie on the kitchen table, where the best natural light was. She pulled out her surgical instruments: a crochet hook, bed pan, old towels and some hot water nearby. I was petrified, feeling really weird, and I couldn't form any words. As she tried to perform the abortion, I felt I was going to die then and there. Never before had I had seen so much blood. On the one hand, she was trying to soothe me, and on the other, she was berating me because it wasn't working properly. As time dragged on, the operation was finally successful, and out came the foetus.

I must have passed out, but by the time I woke up, Aunty Iris and a man in a suit were standing over me, looking worried. Apparently, I had a high fever and was bleeding profusely. For the first time in my life, a doctor was called. I passed out again, but he had given me an injection into my arm and, miraculously, the whole world went black.

It would take me over a week to recover. I had developed severe complications and was so unwell that Nana B made me poached eggs every day for breakfast, an unheard-of treat during my childhood.

Although they tried their best to make sure I never conceived again, I did end up pregnant several more times. Each time, once my pregnancy was confirmed, I would be made to take very hot gin baths. If that wasn't successful in inducing a miscarriage, The Monster would kick me hard in the stomach to dislodge the baby. Sometimes though, abortion was the only option.

Between the ages of eleven and sixteen, Nana B performed three abortions on me, but I will never forget that first one.

During that year when I was turning twelve, darkness further engulfed me, and I withdrew into myself more and more. While the sexual, physical and emotional abuse had previously been shared amongst us girls, it was now all heaped onto me. There were many dark moments during those eighteen months, but the sickest were when The Monster watched the rugby. He liked me to kneel naked with my back positioned like a table-top so he could balance a large beer bottle on my back and watch the game. He also enjoyed inserting the bottle tops into me wherever he could and then rape me at half-time. If I moved an inch, I would be beaten or kicked. He sometimes invited select mates to join in the fun, so while they watched the match, I served as both a table and a sex toy.

After one of the games, a friend of his was nice to me, though not within earshot of my father. This just confused me, because I thought that meant he would take me home with him. Clearly, that wasn't going to happen, as the second my father walked back into the room, he started laughing with him about something.

Rugby nights were not the only awful nights. There were other lengthy, debauched parties where these men had free reign, and I was the sole entertainment for the evening. They thought it was fun to have several of them rape me simultaneously, while the others would egg them on and time them to see how long it took them to ejaculate. Adding to the fun, making it wildly exciting for them, was when they drew straws to see who would get me first, in any way they wanted. It was terrifying, and I often had to crawl out of the lounge as I couldn't walk.

One day, I came home after school to find The Monster standing there, waiting. He was in what I would describe as his 'black mood'. This was the worst of his moods and at the extreme end of his spectrum of vitriolic and cruel behaviour.

Debauchery and depravity usually went hand in hand with whatever scheme he dreamed up. All I knew was that as darkness descended, the fear in me spiked. Although I was skilled as a chameleon and knew how to manipulate the best out of him, on those 'black mood' days nothing worked.

This day was no exception. I had my period, and he knew it.

He followed me into the toilet and watched me change my pad. He then reached in, grabbed the soiled one and told me to go and lie in the hallway. He proceeded to take my clothes off, rubbing the used pad all over them so they became smeared with my blood. Once my clothes were off, he told me to lie back down, stuck two fingers into me and started smearing my blood all over my body. He then reached for my face and did the same thing. My gagging only infuriated him. He was chanting all the while calling me a 'filthy fucking bitch', sticking my fingers into me and then into my mouth, making me suck on them.

But it still wasn't enough. He made me sit up, rip the pad up, eat it shred by shred, and tell him how delicious it was. He kept on and on at this until it was all gone. I ran away crying and threw up everywhere, but he came after me and was just about to make me eat that up too when we heard my brother arrive home with a friend. That seemed to snap him out of his evil state, as he told me to clean up the mess and go to my room. All I can say is that I was glad Shane had brought a friend home with him that day.

Although there was never any rhyme or reason for his behaviour, there was never any escape either.

A few days later, Shane was holding me down on the kitchen floor, farting on my face, when The Monster arrived home. 'You can do better than that,' he said, 'why not shit on her and make her eat it?' So, Shane did just that: made me eat it and then he watched me be violently sick for the next few days.

It was becoming increasingly obvious to me that there were no lines they wouldn't cross when forcing abject humiliation and degradation on me. They were almost competing to see who could come up with the worst horror to put me through. To them, it was a game. To me, it reduced what little humanity I had left until I was just a worthless object. It seemed like the more they put me through, the more it turned into a competition between them to see how much I could take. It was as if nothing would ever be too much for them to try, and it was at that moment that I realised something quite powerful: I couldn't rely on anyone to help me; I could only rely on myself.

This became one of my most significant life lessons and resonated strongly with me. I needed to learn to cope with whatever they did to me and emerge as unscathed and unaffected as possible. They could, and did, do whatever they wanted, physically and emotionally, but there was one part of me they couldn't touch: my mind.

They didn't know it, but I could still find joy in things and admire the beauty in the light outside. Although I usually went to bed crying, I could look at the sky and see the moon. When it was full, I noticed how beautiful it was and that it seemed to be smiling at me, so I would smile back.

The strength of my mind and spirit became my saviour. I could go there any time and connect, whilst holding on fiercely to the hope that gave me. This is what saved me in the end.

MINI ME

My brother's life continued to be privileged and was so entirely different to mine that it was like comparing black to white. He was spoiled rotten and could do what he liked. He got whatever he wanted, expecting it and viewing it as normal. Everything was freely given to him and eventually demanded by him. Had his needs not been met instantly, it would have been somewhat of a surprise to us all. I, on the other hand, was expected to cook, clean and wash clothes as well as wait on both of them hand and foot. It didn't seem to matter that Shane was four years older than me and The Monster was an adult.

Being the only female made everything my job and I became fully responsible for running the household. Being eleven meant I didn't really have a clue about what I was doing and was completely overwhelmed. I didn't understand that I should only use hot water to make sure the dishes got cleaned properly, or that if I used the wringer washing machine, I had to rinse the clothes after washing them. I had no idea that you had to scrub vegetables before you cooked them, or that meat needed seasoning. How was I to know? I had never been taught to cook, let alone to clean and do the washing. It was dispiriting and miserable and I was always so exhausted and overwhelmingly out of my depth.

My relationship with Shane, although never good, was to be irreversibly destroyed. At the start of our new lives living with my father, Shane would sometimes leave me alone and just ignore me. Over time, this changed to him constantly setting me up, so I would either be in trouble with, or beaten by, my father. I struggled with his apparent hatred of me, as I never felt I had done anything to deserve it. I came to recognise that he had an emotionally detached bully living inside of him. I slowly realised that he just didn't care and if he had to have anything to do with me, it was to humiliate or hurt me. I felt confused, afraid and very isolated. While other girls at school would talk about their families and regale the class with stories of outings and happy times, I didn't have any such experiences to share. It was torturous for me when they recounted these positive memories, as I would try and anxiously search my mind for anything I could make up to tell them, so I could be part of their world. I thought that if I appeared similar to them, they would see me as one of them and accept me in their lives.

Feeling as isolated as I did, I needed to belong somewhere. As my home was dangerous, and the house where my mother and sisters lived was a place of rejection, these school friends were my only option to find some form of community. I became quite adept at reading their body language and noticing how I could become of interest to them. I learned very quickly who their leader was and adapted my style to appeal to her specifically. It seemed to work; the only problem being that I had to remember what I had told her, as most of it was lies and I couldn't afford to be caught out in one. The girls knew I had an older brother and in fact one of them had a brother at the same school and year as him, so she would talk to me about them. I knew she wanted to come over to my house, but I also knew it wasn't safe for her or, more importantly, for me, because I couldn't have anyone see the conditions in which I lived. It was too dismal and embarrassing, let alone that I was fearful of what Shane and his friends might subject her to. I struggled to find ways to keep her at bay, when all I really wanted was a close friend who I could have some fun and spend time with. Anything to take me out of the miserable existence I seemed destined to endure.

For some reason, the more I tried to put her off, the more interested she became in him. I couldn't tell her that if she ever saw my reality, or how I was treated, she would be gone from my life. In the end I lied and said he already had a girlfriend. She seemed to accept that, but it meant many more questions from her and lies from me, and so the friendship slowly came to an end.

As the days and weeks dragged by, I would wander home long after the school bell had rung, hoping no one would be there, so I could at least have some sleep or sneak some food. My father had decreed that if he wasn't there, I was required to ask Shane's permission before I could eat or drink anything. Those days meant that if he came home and saw a glass or plate on the bench, evidence that I had eaten or drunk something, he would report me to my father, or find a way to punish me himself. He had been instructed by The Monster to 'educate' me in the proper way for women and girls to behave in this world. Even more than that, Shane was constantly encouraged to do anything he could to belittle and hurt me and eventually it became apparent he was being conditioned to become The Monster's 'mini me'.

My here and now became surviving not one, but two abusers who took great pleasure in extracting as much suffering and pain from me as they could. They always reduced me to nothing, as that was what seemed to give them the greatest pleasure, having me beaten and submissive. However, while they could physically hurt me, they could never reach into my soul where the light shone through regardless, and for that I was grateful.

A 'fun' way in which The Monster groomed Shane to taunt me was through my hunger. He would bring home food for dinner, make me set the table for the three of us, then begin eating. If I went to dish some up for myself, he would yell, 'What do you think you are doing? No one said you could eat.' I would sit there, watching them chew while my own empty mouth salivated at the smell, tummy grumbling loudly, feeling faint. On a good day, he would sometimes let me eat once they had finished, but only what they couldn't eat themselves. They had to have stuffed themselves full before I could eat what was left. I was usually not permitted to eat with them, rather I had to wait until after they had finished and then I might be allowed the cold leftovers, or food that Shane had contaminated in some way.

One of my father's favourite tricks was to smear food onto the floor and make me beg for it, then lick it up like a dog. He seemed to enjoy this, especially if I was stripped naked before doing so. He also encouraged my brother to get involved. 'Think of this as a fun game,' my father would tell him. Shane would put a dog collar around my neck and lead me around the house, dragging me to the food and laughing at me trying to eat it. The Monster could and would add variations to this theme, like tying me to a chair and leaving me there till morning. Sometimes he made me bark to communicate, as he cried with laughter at the sight of me, although I think his personal favourite was to chain me up outside and command me to howl at the moon. Because of the way our back deck was covered, no one could see into our property, so I would sometimes be left there for several days. If my father wasn't too drunk or out of it, he would sometimes leave me a water bowl, but I was only ever allowed to lap it up like a dog.

I got used to being 'the dog', whining, howling, or barking, but as time passed, The Monster decided I wouldn't speak at all unless ordered to. It gave him more power over me, and he could objectify me to an even greater level. He would communicate with me by either using a whistle or verbal commands, such as sit, stay and beg. If I mistakenly spoke, I would be kicked or slapped, or worse, so I chose not to and, to be honest, what was the point anyway? As the months went by, Shane grew to love this as well and he began to replicate all of the behaviours my father modelled for him, specifically his cruel and sadistic treatment of me.

This dog behaviour was what he most enjoyed subjecting me to over those eighteen months and an added evil twist was to taunt me and tell me that if I ever had children, they would only be puppies, as a 'bitch' like me was not able to have real children. This was traumatising, as I had recently had an abortion which left me feeling vulnerable and confused. My father could see the impact of his words and started repeating it over and over again, yelling into my face and pulling me up by the dog collar. In that moment, I learned to do something which he never realised. From that day on, I learned to tune out his words and make up my own in my head. In that way, I couldn't really hear what he was saying and, better yet, he couldn't see how I felt. You see, I had finally worked out that it lit him up if he saw how much I was struggling with his debasement and cruelty of me, so I chose to take that away. Looking back, it was all quite simple and in my child like way I began to take charge. Even when I was not ordered to, I began to stop speaking in his presence unless requested to. He thought he was in control, but in fact it was me choosing not to speak to him. He was too arrogant and obtuse to see it, but I knew, and knowing gave me an even greater sense of my own power. Power in a situation where I had none gave me hope, and that hope was what I clung onto.

My kindest view of Shane was that he had little choice in the matter of how he treated me. The more realistic view was that he always had a choice when we were alone, so as a result of him opting to act in a sadistic and cruel manner towards me, I hated and feared him in equal measure. He could have been kind to me when The Monster wasn't there, he could have given me some food, he could have looked out for me. But he chose not to. Whatever he told himself, however he rationalised it, he knew what he was doing. He knew the truth of his behaviour and the impact it had on me, and with that knowledge he chose to ignore me, taunt me, hurt me, abuse me or trick me, laughing whilst doing so. It seemed The Monster had taught him well.

Life went on and I became ever more hypervigilant, never letting my guard down. I never forgot the day that one of The Monster's friends came round, caught me in the kitchen and asked if I was okay. I wasn't. I was worn out, with all of the household chores, the abuse, my schoolwork. I was simply surviving—lonely, scared and highly anxious. I was a child sex slave, completely trapped with no means of escape. That was in the early 1970s in New Zealand, which was then, and still is now, widely regarded as being one of the safest places in the world. All it would have taken to break the cycle of abuse was for one person to speak out. Had any one of those adults in my life spoken to the police, then potentially, I could have been removed from that house of horrors. For whatever reason, it didn't happen. That was not my path.

During this time, and with my father's unending encouragement, Shane's friends started abusing me as well. Although only fifteen years old at the time, they began experimenting sexually on me, which eventually took on a more sinister tone. While they were only four years older than me, these boys were much bigger, stronger and more powerful, and escape was impossible. Because of what Shane had experienced living under

The Monster's mentorship, he saw it as natural for him to encourage his friends' participation in abusing me. What was sad for me was that, until that point, I had thought they were our family friends. We used to play in the street just a few years earlier.

When it started, I tried to avoid them as much as I could, but each day I was faced with an ultimatum of getting a hiding for not being home in time to cook tea for my father or being raped by three boys after school. I began to accept that I was just an object for anyone who wanted to use me and that there was no end to the horror I would have to keep enduring. I wished they would just leave me alone, but Shane's behaviour towards me only worsened. A low point during that time was when the boys played a poker game, and I was the prize. It's one thing to tease your little sister. It's another thing entirely to rape, sodomise and share her with your friends.

I used to run down to the phone box at night and call the police. I did this on several occasions, but once I had dialled through, I was always too scared to actually speak to them. In a panicked instant, I would hang up, run home, then run back again and try again, only to hang up in wordless fear. I even rang from home a few times, but I was terrified as I knew my father could talk his way out of anything he wanted to. People liked him, tended to think he was a great guy and, to my mind, believed his every word. I, on the other hand, was an unreliable witness—always in trouble at school, known as a troublemaker in the neighbourhood and therefore, unbelievable. I learned that adults tended to trust other adults' words, so there was no point in using mine.

I didn't stand a chance. I remember during one of the school holidays when my brother had his friends around and they were playing Black Sabbath in his bedroom really loudly, I tried to hide away from them and the noise, but they tracked me down. I had hidden in the spare room under the bed, but they found me, dragged me out from underneath, pulled off my clothes and made me parade around in front of them before they took turns raping me. I was distraught, as by then I had developed a crush on one of Shane's friends. I was embarrassed, scared and humiliated and just wanted the ground to swallow me up. I was made to stay there that whole day. As it was during the school holidays, there was no respite since my father's instructions had been that Shane was in charge and I had to stay home.

I began to steal even more money to buy food and cigarettes, as I had taken up smoking. I also found myself lying and causing trouble, adopting any maladaptive behaviours I could to feel as though I were getting away with something. If I could get away with something, it meant I was alive; if I was alive, I had a choice; if I had a choice, I could do this. It became a secret of mine to steal as much as I could, spend it on smokes or treats and feel as if I had something all to myself that they knew nothing about. That was my power, or so I thought. Alongside my Angels, it gave me some courage that I could survive this day and then the next.

The community surrounding us seemed to have no interest in what was going on in our house after my parents' separation, specifically during that time. Years after the fact, one neighbour commented to me that it was so unusual that the gates were always shut. Another mentioned that they always wondered what was going on in that house. But at the time, the church, the neighbours, the tennis club and family friends never asked any questions of my parents.

At the time when my parents separated, it was unusual for people to divorce, especially members of the Catholic Church. People may have wondered about our family, but this was an era of 'mind your own business' and from local authorities down, power was delegated to the man of the house to run his own family the way he saw fit. When my mother left the family home, her subsequent neglect and abandonment of her children were significant in two ways. The first of these was that it ensured her complete disinterest in me, as I didn't see her much, and if it hadn't been for keeping up a certain 'perception' in the community, I firmly believe I would never have seen her again. So, it's not remarkable that she chose not to pay any attention to me, let alone advocate for me. Secondly, in those days, for the father to have custody of children, let alone a pubescent girl as young as I was, was remarkable in its uniqueness.

What is astounding is that the wider community sensed something wasn't right yet did nothing. Decades later, a friend of the family confided that he did not like my father's treatment of us girls. Specifically, he had seen him lining us up outside on the lawn and kicking us like we were footballs, trying to see what distance he could cover.

Despite witnessing this first-hand and feeling that palpable sense of discomfort, the 'friend' did nothing. This seemed to be the period where people noticed things, commented quietly and continued with their own lives. At least in my case.

In this day and age, I can only hope that we are collectively so much more sensitive to the abuse of children, that the perpetrators would be quickly reported, hauled off to jail, and the children sent somewhere safe where neither parent could hurt them again. That would have been my version of heaven, but sadly it was not to be.

CHOICE

I had now been living with my father and brother for about eight months and school became my safe haven. Although those friends I had made at school were a welcome distraction from my home life, they never really knew me. They got to know and play with the girl I showed them. I became very good at putting on a false front which I strongly identified with, partly because they seemed to like it, but mainly because I couldn't afford to reveal too much about myself out of fear. Fear of them discovering that I was not the person I pretended to be at school.

Even more than that, I felt shame, such deep shame that my life was so different to everyone else's and that no matter how hard I tried, I couldn't be like them. Their reality was in such contrast to mine. They lived in clean and warm houses filled with the smell of home-cooked meals, with parents who loved them. I lived in a dirty, smelly and evil house where monsters lived, and no child was safe. It just wasn't possible for me to open that door to anyone, as no one would understand, and my shame was greater than any friendship anyway. If I put it to the test, the shame would outlast them all.

The real me was sad, confused and felt such a deep sense of isolation that it threatened to drown me. Had I shown that to anyone, I don't believe it would have helped, so my false self stayed firmly in place until that is who I eventually identified with. It had worked well with my parents, so why not with my friends from school?

What I did have working for me endlessly was the power of my mind—my courage and my ability to transcend. These were given to me, compliments of my Angels. The enormous resilience I needed to find, the light I needed to see, the ocean of love I needed to feel was all there in my mind and heart and always wrapped in Angels' wings. They sat with me, looked after me and encouraged me when there was nothing left in me and I wanted to press 'end'. They seemed to have a way of knowing this and would send me signs that I was so desperate to see that I could almost feel them before they appeared. If the moon was bright, I would find an upside-down Angel; if the stars came out, I saw a magical fairyland where kindness and horses lived. They believed in me, stood by me and made sure I was okay. When I had to face another bout of abuse or violence from The Monster, I knew I always had the light to look to, so that's where I would go—into the light.

During that year, parents were required to attend parent-teacher conferences at school, and I knew I was in more trouble than usual, as it was, after all, only several months since my parents had separated and I had been acting out badly. I knew my father would be told how badly behaved I was and, although I had already figured the consequence would be a hiding or having to sleep outside for a few days, I was still nervous as to how he might react. My behaviour at school had deteriorated so much that I was usually sent to the bench outside the classroom, after being strapped by Sister Helena. I was trying desperately to get her to notice me, to see the sad and broken child inside, who had bruises and marks that couldn't really be accounted for, that was always crying out for attention. But she didn't get it. Occasionally, she would ask me what was going on with me, but the secret was too great and the fear a tsunami, threatening to engulf not just me, but everyone else if they even had a sense of it. So, I just played up, called out, and was rude, disobedient and cheeky.

In the end, it got so bad that I was sent out of the classroom more than I was in it. I know my friends wondered why I was always so attention-seeking, but I had no choice, I had to survive this and if it meant getting noticed, then it was all worth it.

Sister Helena must have been some sort of saint as she never made me feel bad about myself. Instead, she was always kind and compassionate towards me and I know that's why I was so desperate for her to notice what was wrong and to save me. But she never did. Child abuse was simply not on her radar. It would be decades later, when she told me she had always thought something was wrong at home. Further, that if she had known then what she knew now, sexual abuse would have been her first guess. I don't know what she said to my father that night at the interviews, but I didn't get a hiding and I didn't get punished, so maybe something in her realised it wouldn't be good to tell him the truth.

Maybe she had tried to protect me after all.

Even though the most overwhelming emotion I felt during that time was isolation, that was not all I was destined to feel, as it was that year that joy materialised in my life in the form of netball. Before then, I had no idea how wonderful the game was, or of the thrill I would feel playing it. Tossing the ball high up into the air, intercepting a pass or shooting a goal felt incredible. The feel of the ball in my hands and the sound of the swish of the net released something in me that was usually not around—excitement. Even better, we had a basketball hoop attached to the garage at home, simply because Shane had wanted one. We also had a ball, and whenever I could, I was out there putting up shots. I would put up maybe five hundred a day, which took me out of myself and gave me something I seemed to be able to master.

This was at a time when goal shooters on the team were only able to shoot with one hand (whereas now, players tend to use both hands while shooting) so that was how I trained, and a nice surprise came when I realised that I was actually quite good. I ended up representing the school always as the goal shooter. We used to play other schools on certain days and that became the highlight of my life up to that point. It was exciting, fun and so rewarding that I almost forgot my life was my life and felt joy—real joy—for the first time since my mother had abandoned me.

One Friday night, The Monster received a call asking if I could come and fill in for an older team who played on Saturdays. They were playing in a competition round and their shooter had fallen sick. For some reason I will never understand, he said yes. In retrospect, he was probably put on the spot and, being the true psychopath he was, had to convince people he was 'Mr Charm and Personality'. Whatever the reason, this was like three Christmases come at once for me. I was elated to be chosen to play for an older team, and that my father had let me. I went down on that Saturday and played the game of my life. I was so excited that I intercepted passes, shot goals and impressed the older girls who wanted me on their team.

Of course, I had to find my own way there and back, but that weekend kept me going for weeks to come. It was what I would relive when the abuse and fear got too much. I told myself that if I could keep playing netball, I could cope with anything and life would be worth living. I was hopeful that if I just focused on netball and school, I would get through each day. Because I was reasonably good at the sport, I was getting some positive reinforcement from other people. Not only the nuns, but also the girls in my netball team would congratulate me on my shooting skill. I loved it, relishing the recognition for something I had earnt, and I felt confident every time I shot my next goal. Immersed in that feeling of being validated and 'seen', I never wanted the school week to end.

Even though I longed for companionship and friendship from other kids in the neighbourhood and at school, I tried very hard not to get too close to them. It wasn't safe for me or them, so I kept them at bay, but I hadn't counted on Michelle. I first met her through a school camp. She lived about a twenty-minute walk away from my home and I just loved hanging out with her. We used to laugh at the same things, like the same cartoons and just have fun. She ended up becoming a very close friend and it wouldn't be too long, as with everything else good in my life, that the friendship would come to an end. In the meantime, though, she became someone I would often hang out with and the only friend I ever had to the house, only because I couldn't come up with any more excuses to keep her away. I had come up with so many reasons for why she couldn't come over, that she thought I must have another friend I liked better.

If only that had been the case.

That first day she was due to come over after school, I got up early and made sure the house was as clean as I could make it and checked my stolen money pile so I could buy us treats at the dairy on the way home. I had been given permission for her to be there, so I wasn't unduly worried when my father turned up. The first visit seemed fine. The

Monster was pleasant to her and acted in a friendly manner towards me for the few hours she was there. Subsequent visits also seemed to go surprisingly well, and he was on his best behaviour whenever she was around. I thought it was great as—we used to shoot hoops together and play silly games. I was sometimes allowed to go to her house, and I got quite good at getting her to ask The Monster if I could go and play there. On the days he agreed, I felt as though I was almost living a different life. Almost.

One day, The Monster asked when Michelle would be coming around next and encouraged me to invite her to play at our house. I thought it was so cool. Not only could she come and play, but he would even let her stay for dinner and drop her home later. We arranged a day and I skipped home from school, excited about telling her about a boy I thought was cute. Soon after she arrived, The Monster turned up and I thought nothing of it, it wasn't that odd for him to come home for a tea break, but what was odd was he was carrying treats. I immediately felt worried. I thought to myself, what was going on? Why did he have treats with him?

As the afternoon wore on, he sat down with us and wanted to join in our game, asking Michelle to show him how to play. Then, he put his hand on her leg. I immediately felt sick and tried to get him to stop. He told me not to be silly and that they were just playing. Michelle didn't know what was happening, but I did. I started feeling more and more anxious because I could see he was grooming her and that if I didn't intervene, I knew what was coming next. I started to panic and couldn't wait for her to be taken home. Somehow, a part of me knew with absolute certainty that I had to get her out of there, or at least be in the van and sit in the middle when he drove her home so he couldn't touch her.

As night fell, I started to make comments about how I was tired and how Michelle's mum would be expecting her home. The Monster said she would be fine and that her mum knew where she was. I kept making comments and finally he told me to 'stop whining'. Michelle, of course, was none the wiser, and after what seemed like an eternity, our afternoon was finally over, and she was expected home. The problem was that he would not let me go with them. He told me it was time for me to get ready for bed and that she would be fine with him. I felt sick with worry—there was no way I wanted her left alone with him. I started pleading to join them, but he wouldn't listen. I managed to grab Michelle while he got the keys and whispered, 'Please ask if I can come with you.' She agreed and asked, 'Can Gloria come too?' so he had to choose, and luckily he uttered a reluctant 'yes'. I had gone against his plan and he was not happy.

When we dropped her off, he told me to stay in the van while he walked her to the door. I watched in horror, seeing him fondle her backside as she walked in. Oh my God, what could I do? How could I ever have her again at our house? It wasn't safe. I heard him tell her mum that she was welcome to stay the night next time, perhaps over a weekend.

I didn't sleep that night. I was sick with worry about what he had in store for Michelle. If she came back, I knew he would start abusing her and I couldn't let that happen. Over the next few weeks, I panicked and fretted. It was all up to me. I tried to think about what I could do that would work; I even wrote it down. My options boiled down to only seeing her at her house, only playing with her when he was out, pretending that I wasn't allowed to invite her over, or pretending that I didn't like her anymore so that the friendship would end. Selfishly,

I didn't want to pick the last option as I really liked Michelle and the friendship we had formed. The problem was if I tried to just see her at her house, she would be upset with me and wonder why. I couldn't tell her why. The secret had to be kept. But if I didn't have her back at our house, The Monster would make me invite her over. After what felt like a month of torture, I made a decision. The only option was to end the friendship.

Something inside me broke as I started to pretend I didn't like her anymore by avoiding seeing her or seeking her out. She kept phoning me to talk and sent me letters, but I couldn't risk it. I didn't want her hurt. It would make me responsible and I couldn't do that to her. So, I acted as if she meant nothing to me and ignored any attempts, she made. One day, she phoned me crying. I felt dreadful, but what else could I do? She didn't ring the next day or the day after that.

About a week later, her mother phoned and asked The Monster why I was doing this and why I didn't want to be friends with her daughter anymore. The Monster came and asked me what was going on. The reality was that I had no words, as there wasn't anything I could say that would make the situation any better or safer for Michelle. He kept pushing me on this, so I lied and said I didn't like her anymore. He was not happy, telling me that there would be trouble and I would be made to pay for this. The hard truth was that my friendship needed to end, otherwise Michelle would end up like me.

That choice pulled me into a deeper pit of misery and despair. It was awful. But once again, there was no relief or comfort for me. With my Angels, I was able to rationalise my pain and suffering, as I knew she was safe and unhurt, and for that I was grateful. I just didn't want that on my conscience. After all, everything and every other issue that ever surfaced in that house was blamed on me, so why not add saving another child from being hurt and abused as well?

The load I carried for months later almost undid me. Looking back, I see what a strong sense of responsibility and accountability I had. Unasked for, unwarranted and far more than any child should ever have to endure. I came to the realisation that I didn't have a childhood. I was in the body of a child, but really, I couldn't and didn't enjoy the natural delights and joy in life that children should expect to have.

That was taken from me.

When the Monster had said I would be made to pay, I didn't realise just how costly it would be. He planned it well, so as to impact me as painfully as possible. He first took me with him to get a Christmas tree and told me I could help decorate it that night. I was lulled into a false sense of excitement by the idea of it.

Later that night, once it was decorated and the lights were flickering, he tied me to the Christmas tree and raped me with the branches and pinecones while yelling abuse. He made sure I was tied up tightly and told me he was going to bed and that if I moved, he would know, and he would kill me. He then kicked me in the face, urinated into my mouth and proceeded to go to bed. In the morning when he came into the lounge, he was furious I was still there, as couldn't remember what he had done. He called me a 'fucking lying whore' and yelled at me to 'clean yourself up' as we were due at Nana B's house. As I limped out of the room, I smiled to myself—I had a secret.

What he didn't realise was that all through the night I had focused on the fairy at the top of the tree. Her beautiful angelic face and wings seemed to shimmer throughout that long period of time, surrounding me with love and light. She had given me comfort and hope, plus I knew Michelle was safe.

From that point on, anyone who ever wanted to include me in their lives was kept firmly away from me. The dilemma was that I was desperately lonely and isolated and could have done with a friend, but the truth was I couldn't allow it. It broke my heart, but I had to live with myself, so my existence became even more torturous and lonely. Really, I had no choice. It was the right thing to do.

MIRACLE

I had been living with my father for eighteen months and life continued in its now familiar pattern. I still went to my mother's house every second weekend and felt the same disinterest and rejection from her, but it was always reassuring to see my sisters' faces. Those weekends were hard but bearable because at least I knew I could sleep safely without fear of being raped or beaten. When my mother would take me home to my father, I would begin that transition by cleaning up their mess from the weekend and doing their washing and cooking for them. My world would suddenly dial up from ten to a hundred in fear and intensity. At least the cleaning gave me focus and a slight sense of calm.

I had learned to become more of a mistress to The Monster than anything else, working overtime to ensure both my safety and survival. The best outcomes for me were when he was less angry and violent, so even though I disliked and feared him, I learned to manipulate him as much as I could, I learned how to become his lover and knew exactly how to please him to ease my suffering. I am not sure how I knew to develop this subterfuge; it was pure instinct, but I was desperate to be as safe as I could so my coping mechanisms had to be continually evaluated and improved. I worked out ways to make him feel more of a man, told him I loved him, that I was so happy to be with him, basically anything I could to save myself from his nasty and cruel abuse. I must have been convincing, as he eventually decided it would be good for me to move from my room into his.

That was when I began to see moments of care and interest being shown towards me. Shane sensed the change in him and was not happy about it. In response, he chose to ramp up the nastiness towards me, but it didn't work, as I had something The Monster craved above all else: a twelve-year old's body. The deeper part of me knew that if I kept providing him with everything he wanted, he might be nicer.

I convinced myself I had this covered and that if I kept going with my plan, it meant I would get through each day okay. However, life didn't stay the same, and what happened next was the first miracle I ever experienced.

It was a school day, and we were finishing at midday as the teachers were having a planning afternoon. I reluctantly walked home to see the van in the driveway. My heart sank and I started to tremble. I quietly walked in hoping not to call any attention to myself, but I could hear voices coming from the bedroom. I went down the hallway wondering who it was and why they were in the bedroom. I looked in and there was The Monster in bed, naked, with a woman. I turned and ran. I didn't know where I was going, but I ended up at my mother's house. I was shaken up and traumatised.

The feelings I had were so overwhelming—I was devastated. In my shocked state, I didn't understand what I had seen, or any part of it at all. I had mistakenly believed that as I was his mistress, he wouldn't need anyone else. He had said so many things to me about us being together forever, how he would always love me and how special I was to him. Things I had believed and held onto, as they meant that maybe he truly loved me after all. I was so proud of myself for having been promoted from slave to mistress that I had not figured there would be another who could provide what I was to him. I had channelled so much energy and hope into pretending I liked what he did to me, I had almost convinced myself.

I had also done much to ensure I anticipated his every need. I had mistaken his manipulation as love, and as I was so desperate to get any love I could, seeing him with another woman broke me. I thought my chameleon strategy had worked, I thought I had mastered the situation. He had even begun talking to me sometimes, especially if I pre-empted what he may want or need. He would sometimes treat me well and I lived for those moments, as they helped me feel a connection with him that I didn't have with anyone else. I needed love and kindness and if it was only going to come from him, I craved it, no matter how small the amount, in whatever form it took.

These were only rare moments, but they were enough that I felt my life could be worth something, mean something, and I could hopefully have some sort of happiness. Seeing a woman in his bed shattered that illusion and left me feeling replaced and betrayed. Incoherent thoughts spun in my mind as I ran in shock and grief to my mother.

Her house was some four kilometres away and I was a mess when I finally arrived, sobbing, struggling to breathe and clinging to her. Maybe something different showed on my face because, for the first time in my life, she chose to comfort me while I shared what I had seen. She was still for a while, before questioning me over and over for what felt like hours before letting me stay the night. I was exhausted, unhinged and fell into a deep sleep. She apparently got on the phone, talked to a priest and told him what had happened. She phoned other people that night and was apparently told the same thing by all of them: 'Get her out of his house, it is morally wrong for her to be there.'

I was still in shock the next morning when she questioned me again about what happened and then informed me that I would have to live with her and that what he had done was had broken one of the ten commandments: 'Thou shalt not commit adultery.' Apparently, it was okay for a child to be repeatedly raped, viciously beaten and sold into child sex slavery, but it was frowned upon for a man to commit adultery, which was what the Catholic Church considered he was doing. On that basis, it was not 'seemly' for me to remain in his care. The disbelief and joy almost felt too good to be true. I broke down and just wept and wept.

Thank you, my Angels. Had that woman not been there that day, I would have remained living with him. But, as with everything else about my mother, there was a cost. I knew deep down she still didn't want me with her, but she had no choice as once she had spoken to the priest, her hands were tied, and she had to take me in. She decided there was a condition attached to her generosity. The only way she would remove me from his care was if I would go back into his house and tell him by myself that I wanted to leave and live with her. I had to face him alone and tell him I didn't want to be with him anymore.

I was terrified, as I didn't want to see him again, let alone tell him that. She was adamant that either I did it that way or I wouldn't be able to move out. All the way down to his place, I begged her, cried and pleaded with her to at least come in with me, but she refused and finally she told me, 'Be quiet and grow up, you got what you wanted.' She drove into his driveway and refused to get out of the car, forcing me to go in and face him alone. I knew if I didn't go in and tell him face to face, I would never escape him. This really was my only chance at leaving him and the hell in which he had imprisoned me.

The suffering, abuse and torture I had sustained at his hands felt like nothing next to the courage I had to find to face him alone with the truth that I didn't want to be with him anymore.

As a child, this was the hardest thing I had ever done in my life. Confronting The Monster alone was like facing the devil himself. My mother was fully aware of this, as she sat in the driveway, impatiently waiting for me to get on with it. Once again, she left me to it. The anxiety and fear crashed in on me as I walked into his house and told him I wanted to live with her. He sat in his armchair, looked at me and said, 'What's all this, then?' He refused to believe I didn't want to be there with him anymore and tried to bribe me to stay, but I was wiser. Even though I was traumatised and fearful, I stood my ground. He turned nasty and told me I wouldn't last a week with her and that when I did come back to see him, he wouldn't be the nice dad he had been. I walked out, ran to the car, threw myself in it and started crying. Only then did my mother get out of the car, go to the door and have a furtive conversation with him. I was to learn later, that discussion sealed my fate until my sixteenth birthday.

Once we were on the way to her house, I was beside myself. On the one hand, I was upset and still scared, and on the other, thrilled, as I would be finally living with Mum and my sisters away from the horror.

I was excitedly babbling about where I would sleep until she revealed that I would still have to see him—every second weekend, that he would still have access. I told her I couldn't go back there. Coldly and bluntly, she informed me that the Catholic Church and the judge didn't think his access should be completely denied. Despite this remark, I am sure it was my mother who decided this for me. The irony was if the Catholic Church decided it was unsafe for me to be there alone with him full-time, why would two days out of fourteen be considered safe, especially consecutively over a weekend? Nevertheless, and thanks to my Angels, I was free of him for twelve out of fourteen days. That felt like a miracle to me, one that I truly believe saved my life.

The first access weekend I was due to spend with The Monster had me feeling anxious and afraid. I knew he was furious with me because I'd left and I was sure he would make me pay, I just didn't know how.

It was not unusual for him to host big sex parties from home and charge a fee for men to use me. When I arrived that first weekend, I was scorned, ridiculed and told I had made a big mistake. He came up close, pulled my hair and dragged me into my old bedroom, which he then proceeded to barricade. He yelled at me that I was under no circumstances to leave that room, and if I tried, he would know and smash my head in. I would have been too afraid to leave it anyway, but he made sure I knew he would hear me if I tried to escape.

Overnight, and through most of the next day, I was left in there. I was too scared to sleep, as then I couldn't protect myself and I couldn't get out to use the toilet, so in the end I had to use the wardrobe as my bathroom. I felt ashamed and dirty, but too scared to call attention to myself. Around 4 pm the next day, I heard noises at the door, and he came in telling me to get myself cleaned up, that he had friends coming and I better do what they said, otherwise he would lock me back in the room. I went into the bathroom, ran the bath, cleaned myself up and went back to the room. He came in with a drink and some pills, watched me take them and then told me, 'You better be sexy for my friends.' I felt sick and weak, as I hadn't eaten since lunch the day before, but as that would have been laughed at or ignored, I didn't bother saying anything.

It was getting dark when the men began arriving. I recognised most of them as they had been regulars at our home. I had been given an outfit to wear with feathers and a shimmery short dress which was too big for me, but I had to wear it, so I did the best I could. As I walked into the hallway, I focused on the pattern in the carpet; it had flowers on it, and I liked flowers. As I approached the lounge, I could hear the men talking and laughing and felt even more afraid. My father came out, told me I better do a good job and then I was pushed into the room. Beer flowed, music played, and I was told to 'get those hips moving' to try and look sexy for the men. I felt nothing but knew it would go better for me if I pretended that I was loving every minute of it. As I swayed seductively to the music, my father gave each man a numbered card and told them this represented the order they would abuse me in.

The energy in the room shifted and I could see the excitement on their faces. He told them to settle down as before they could touch me, they needed to give over the money. While I kept dancing and moving to the music the monster explained the rates to them. He said he had a special rate for 'anything goes', another for straight sex and yet another for sodomy. There was even a 'super special' if two of them wanted a go at the same time. Meanwhile, twelve-year-old me kept dancing, trying as hard as I could to switch off to what was coming. The music was turned up, the money put away and they began to touch me while

I was dancing. I secretly begged my Angels to stay with me.

As the night unfolded and they got more and more drunk, The Monster came up with a bizarre suggestion. As he had lots of tools in his van, he thought they should try using them on me. The others looked surprised, thought he was joking and when they realised, he wasn't, got up to help him. I watched out of the window as they began retrieving them from the back of the van. I saw poles, wrenches and screwdrivers among them. being delivered into the room. At one point I asked The Monster if I could go to the toilet. I was terrified; my heart was beating so fast and I don't know what gave me the courage, but I decided to run. I raced into my bedroom, got my bag and snuck out the back door.

Outside, it was pitch black and there weren't many cars on the road. My mother's house seemed a long way away, but I had to escape and had nowhere else to go. In the middle of the night, it was not safe for me to be out alone, but I had no choice—it was safer for me there than back in The Monster's house. As I sprinted down the road, I was terrified they were coming after me. If I saw headlights coming, I hid behind trees and cars in case they were hunting me down. I also couldn't run in what I was wearing, so I hid behind some bushes, got some clothes out of my bag and hurriedly threw them on. I put the shimmery dress and feather boa into my bag, as I was not going to risk throwing them away, and kept running. Two or three times, I could swear I sensed them coming up the road behind me. It was slow going as I had to keep to the trees and verges as much as I could. By the time I arrived at Mum's, the lights were off, and everything was quiet and still, so I crept into the back of her car and slept there. I was still scared, but I felt a bit safer, as at least I was nowhere near those tools or those men. I didn't even consider waking her, as she would have just been annoyed at me and probably taken me straight back there.

The next morning, I awoke and knocked on the back door to have my sister Debbie answer it. She wanted to know what I was doing there. I told her I felt scared at his house, so came here. When mum woke up and found me there, she was angry at me for having the audacity to ruin the first weekend of my father's access. I tried to say I was scared, but she wouldn't listen. I didn't even bother showing her the clothes The Monster had made me wear, because if she didn't want to know why I was scared, I knew she wouldn't want to know why I was made to dress like that. She let me have breakfast but told me I had to ring my father and get him to come collect me. She wouldn't be taking me there and I should apologise to him for running away.

With a heavy heart and nausea in my stomach, I phoned him and asked him to come and get me. I never wanted to see him again, or be at his house again, but once again my mother handed me to him on a silver platter. No questions asked.

The Monster answered the phone, shouting, swearing and cursing at me. He made me walk back to his house and told me I would be severely punished and that I was a bad ungrateful child. I took as long as I could to walk back, crying all the way with my sister Debbie watching me from the kitchen window.

The positive in it was that even though he raped and beat me, the tools had been packed away and the men were gone.

IMPACT

The impact on me of reuniting with my mother was not what I had imagined. I was so thrilled to be back with her, I just assumed she would be too. It came as something of a shock to realise that, actually, she wasn't. I had never stopped hoping she would love me and long for me the way I did her, but this was not the case. In my mind she would welcome me back, stand up for me and be relieved I was finally back living with her. Sadly, I couldn't have been more mistaken.

After her 'big stand' on getting me out of my father's house, she had no choice but to honour what the Catholic Church advised, when the last thing she wanted was another child to look after. While through the Church's, and her family's, eyes she was seen as something of a hero for saving me from the adulterer, it was hollow as deep down she really didn't want me at all. To her credit, she didn't bother to hide the fact, nor did she make me feel part of the girl's lives, in fact I was made to feel like I owed her in some way. It was bizarre and surreal and not at all how I longed for it to be. I just wanted my mum.

What was so wrong with me that my own mother didn't want me? I felt wrong, bad and exhausted. I didn't have any energy left in me to be devastated or heartbroken, so I just stuffed my feelings down and carried on using my trusted sidekicks: the false self and 'the carer' role I had mastered. I felt they worked well, so to realise that she had always viewed me as 'the bad one' in the family was an unwelcome shock. Unsurprisingly, as unloved children do, I began to fit the role assigned to me. I didn't think I was a bad child, but on some level I believed

I must be, as why else would the people who were meant to love me, dislike me and reject me so easily? Being blamed, misunderstood and resented hurt deeply. I felt as though wherever I was, and whoever I was with, saw me as 'the problem'.

There was nowhere to take this or work it through; I just felt very alone, lonely and wrong. I also realised I'd created a fantasy where my mother was happy to have me back with her once again. That had been what kept me going through the dark days living with my father, when all I wanted was for my life to end. The shocking truth of it was that she resented me even more than he did. Surprising as it sounds, even knowing she didn't want me, I was safe, I was warm, there was food and part of me could relax a little.

As for my sisters, I had been secretly hoping they would have been excited to have me back with them, but they just weren't. When I had visited every second weekend, they were pleasant enough towards me, probably because I was only there for two nights, whereas having me there permanently became a whole other reality to adjust to. Practically speaking, it meant finding me a permanent bed and space in which to sleep. I guess it also meant my mother's attention had to be shared out amongst the three of us, and they didn't get much of it as it was. Not in a genuinely loving way anyway. They were just disinterested, trying to find their own way through the minefield that having a narcissistic mother was. I felt not only that I wasn't believed, but that there was no real concern shown for me around what I'd gone through with my father. In the end, I learned to do what I always did and shut down. Even though I was devastated and traumatised, there was no room for that in either of my sister's lives. They had their own trauma to deal with and didn't want to take on mine. They weren't equipped to manage my fear and grief. Hell, they hadn't even begun to process their own.

My mother, on the other hand, made it abundantly clear that I was welcome there as long as I had no expectations of her for pretty much anything. I needed to learn quickly how to adapt, so adapt I did. Partly, that meant learning not to ask for or demand anything, but the continued rejection was confusing. I suffered as I felt like the odd one out, being viewed with pity rather than love. In their house, alliances had already been formed, while I was on the fringe. When the separation occurred eighteen months earlier, they had established their own ways of being and coping and I was clearly seen as just another demand on their time and resources.

My mother, in particular, had a way of making me feel wrong and bad for even approaching her, so I learned quickly not to bother. I felt alone and abandoned by her. In every way she could, she showed me what a nuisance I was. If I was the first one home from school, she needed rest, if I needed her to sign anything for me, it was almost too much for her. If I wanted money, she told me to ask my father. Basically, it was fine as long as I was doing the giving not the taking. I hadn't considered I would be so traumatised, but I was. I was hyperactive, hyper anxious and hypervigilant around everyone. I would hear noises where there were none and I would wake at night with a fright. I would jump at the sound of a car that sounded like my father's coming down the road. I would hide behind the bedroom door if the phone rang in case it was him.

For the first six months of living in her house, it seemed as though my mother's world expanded while mine contracted. As she became more well-known and successful in her own life, I became more fearful and needy. No one wanted nor cared about me. My behaviour had regressed so much, I felt anxious if she was out of my sight. I didn't want to leave her side, I wanted to be near her, I wanted to know she was right there, I felt safe if I was around her, or at the very least could hear her, but she didn't understand and wouldn't allow it. She would get annoyed with me, not having the interest or the appetite for a needy abused girl in her household. I learned to go within, spend time with my friends and lie a little more, steal a little more and be a bit naughtier. No one understood me.

The only relief I experienced was when I was with those friends who seemed to like me. But really, it was the 'false self' they were drawn to, the happy, outgoing, girl who was willing to take risks with no thought for the consequences. Inside was a swirling mess of doubt, self-hatred and fear. I didn't let the world see that, as I had been shown many times over that was unacceptable. The child I showed to people was the only version of me anyone wanted to see.

A welcome distraction appeared in the form of starting college, and as I was going to a private Catholic school in Auckland, I was going to have to commute by bus and train. I was excited and nervous and looking forward to making some new friends. I needed a distraction and some fun, and this new phase of my life would become my escape from the reality at either of my parents' houses. At least with friends I could focus on things like netball, exams and sleepovers.

My first few months at school were nerve-racking and although Debbie was there with me, she was older and had her own friends and activities. I didn't mind as I wanted to have a new start somewhere and college seemed as good a place as any. It took me a while, but I loved being there. Hanging out with my new friends was exciting, even doing homework was a welcome escape from the reality of my home life. Surprisingly, I did quite well at school as—the type of trauma I was going through had shut down part of my brain but somehow boosted the part that spurred on my determination to achieve A's and B's during that first year. It also meant I got recognition for doing something right.

It wasn't long before I got a part time job so I could at least have money to go out with friends and buy things for myself. I was able to develop an identity outside of my family, which felt kind of good to me. I was lucky enough to get a part time job at the dairy across the road where things like bread, milk and baked goods were sold. I liked the owners, they were nice people, and I was happy to work for them on weekends and during holidays. It meant money for me, as well as an escape from home. I became someone they could rely on so would often be called in last minute to fill in for others who hadn't shown up. I felt valued and important as they were grateful to me and appreciated my work ethic. They used to give me fresh doughnuts or custard pies as an extra thank you, which I would greedily scoff down. Life outside of either of my parents' houses was my reason for living and if I could maintain that façade and keep the secret, I would be okay.

As the months passed, I felt more neglected and abandoned by my mother and I realised one day that there was simply no room for me in her life. She saw my post-traumatic stress disorder (PTSD) as attention seeking and within a year, she and my sisters were openly calling me 'the black sheep of the family'. I didn't hate my sisters, but I wondered why I never experienced the kindness and love preached to them at church every Sunday.

As much as I felt relief at living back with them, I still had the challenge of facing my father every second weekend. Though psychologically and physically dangerous, in some ways, feeling safe for twelve out of fourteen days and half of the school holidays was even worse, as it would always come to an end and the reality of going to my father's was terrifying. I was fearful, suffered endlessly, couldn't concentrate at school and was always in trouble simply because I had a big secret I couldn't tell anyone, specifically my family. The truth was that my mother needed me to cover up the family abuse as she had an image to maintain. I have come to realise that she seemed to embody many of the traits of a narcissist. As with most narcissists, outward appearances were everything to her and it would cost me dearly if I let any part of her carefully crafted image slip and reveal the darkness underneath. That cost usually came in the form of annihilation and as I had already felt the weight of that, I couldn't bear it again. It was too hard for me.

Ultimately, the secret was easier to keep because then at least I could pretend I did have a mother who loved me. She never once commented on or wondered why I was so different when I had to go to my father's or upon my return. She never once asked how it went, or what we did—it was as though it were another door that only I had the key to.

I learned that I was acceptable to my mother if I spoke only of things she wished to discuss, or if I assisted her in her busy and important life. She had a family to raise and money to earn, but she also had a young daughter who was out of her depth and needing help. As that didn't fit with her image of herself, there was only one option and that was to shut me up, keep me quiet and therefore not allow me to show the suffering and shame I felt. I realised I had to bury the unwanted, broken parts of me very deeply because should they see the light of day, I would be destroyed by her.

Her callous disregard and lack of care shone through and I learned without being told that if I wanted to be with her, this was the only option. Only bring the good, loving, obedient daughter to the surface; ignore and bury deeply the ugly, hurt and damaged one. She wanted no part of that me, there was no room for it and so I did what I needed to. I cut that part off, hoping to be accepted and loved for the 'false self'. That seemed to work, but the other sad, broken part was left in the bottom drawer just waiting to be found. I couldn't risk exposing it, but it would emerge through misbehaviour at school or lying to people. I didn't understand any of it, but I was smart and knew how to adapt. The biggest lesson for me was discovering the deeper truth around silence and cover-ups and that I didn't matter to either parent. Even though the eighteen months of horror was over, I was living in a cell of my own at her house, one of self-loathing and despair.

During this time, hell was still open for business, as every second weekend the abuse, prostitution and torture among my father's groups continued. I had no power over this—I had to go and that was that. The sinking feeling I would get while packing my bag for those weekends almost left me breathless. I would have to either find my own way there from school on a Friday or be picked up by my father. Either way it was huge, and I felt dead inside. The initial greeting would be pleasant, even the first hour. He would look pleased to see me, and then I would realise it was because he was expecting to make some money out of me.

I never knew quite what those weekends would entail but it would usually mean that some of his friends would drop by and rape me, or that I would be trafficked and leased out for a sex show or to a group for the weekend. That could be to any of the various groups he belonged to and sometimes involved other children.

Generally, the men would drink heavily and us children would be drugged. Most of what was expected was straight-forward sex, but some of it involved us doing degrading, humiliating things to each other. Some of the other children would break down, unable to perform and be taken away. The rest of us would just carry on performing. I would sometimes see those children at other events and wonder what their punishment had been for cracking under the pressure. I could only guess, but if their fathers were anything like The Monster, it would have been brutal. When these sessions were underway, I never knew quite what was happening, but I was grateful for the drugs as I could dissociate and go into a blissfully hazy bubble to escape from my reality. I often couldn't remember what was happening from one moment to the next. I knew it was something awful though, as it was with a feeling of dread that I would wake up the next day, sad and confused.

Many times during these incidents, I would hear the men dare each other to do things or outdo each other in some perverted way. I knew The Monster wanted me to outshine and outperform all the other girls, so I would be 'the prize' and men would pay more to have me. Consequently, on the way to these events he would threaten me that if I wasn't the best, I would be punished. This would take the form of a beating, being starved for the rest of the weekend or forced to sleep in the garage. I didn't mind the garage, as at least the distance between us was greater.

During the days spent with him, I would once again be the slave: sex slave, domestic slave and personal slave to both The Monster and Shane. My brother would be indifferent as to whether I was there or not and tended to ignore me, unless he wanted something. Although still my father's favourite, he noticed the attention I got and wasn't happy with it unless I was being hurt. I did wonder if he ever thought about protecting me or stopping my father from hurting me, but nothing ever changed, so that was another pointless fantasy. He was often instrumental in setting me up to be hurt and would laugh out loud if my father fell for it. That way he could watch me get beaten or kicked while having his sadistic needs met.

Although we didn't have a relationship at all really, I did notice he didn't seem to mind me doing all of his washing and cleaning, as I guess otherwise the responsibility would have fallen to him. I also wondered how things were in that house when it was just the two of them. Would my father's rageful moments have been transmitted to Shane in my absence? The honest answer is that I don't know, but I always wondered.

I would count down the minutes to when I could go back to my mother's house and although she never wanted to come and get me, my father would often refuse to take me back. As a result, I would often have to walk the long walk back to her house in Titirangi.

It was during those long and lonely hours that I would begin the transition from the child sex slave my father demanded, to the good Catholic girl my mother expected of me. The paradox was not lost on me, but somewhere in the middle lay the child who was me, the desperate, lonely and unloved girl who just put one foot in front of the other and walked through the nightmare that was her life. The child who left for school every Friday morning was never the same child who arrived back on Sunday night.

GANG

What you are about to read focuses on the ages twelve to sixteen.

Although the abuse I suffered was rife from a very young age, as a teenager my sex trafficking services became highly sought after.

My father's greed led him to involve larger groups and a notoriously violent gang. These new men were scarier than any others I had ever encountered before, intimidating and dangerous. While most people wouldn't have crossed paths with them in day-to-day life, The Monster's hunger for fame, financial gain and his own notoriety meant that I became well-acquainted with them.

Whether his association with them was through his club, his paedophile ring, or his nephew David, I was never told. He had many underworld connections and they just added to the growing list. The Monster was not a gang member himself, just an external pimp. I don't know if he had any ambition to join their ranks, but I could clearly see that he felt a sense of importance in being able to provide them something they wanted.

What became obvious was that at some prearranged meeting, a deal had been made with key gang leaders who decided what I should do, when and to whom. This meant I would attend gang events at certain locations around Auckland and perform the services that had been ordered and paid for.

Although I had suffered much up to this point in my life, nothing could have prepared me for my experiences within the gang. Everything else paled in comparison. I didn't know human beings could behave like that and walk away at peace with their actions. It was so horrific that I would often be in shock and need to be drunk or heavily drugged to cope. There were always at least fifty men there, plus women and children, and I would muster up as much courage as I could and try to be as pleasant as possible so they wouldn't take offence and punch me, kick me, or worse.

Within the gang, there were initiation ceremonies and once someone had been initiated, they were rewarded. The reward took many forms, but over the next year or so, it tended to be me. It was open season, dealer's choice, a choose-your-weapon scenario—they could rape, beat, or kick me half to death, including anyone or anything else they wanted as well. It became competitive too, as whoever came up with the most radical idea received the most attention. However, the most simple and typical act was gang rape and being put on 'the block'. This entailed being spread-eagled onto a slab of wood or concrete with feet and hands tied to each of the four corners. I would be left like that while the queue of gang members waiting to rape me grew longer.

Simply put, these were the most terrifying men I had ever encountered. They were of all shapes and sizes, mainly of New Zealand European or Māori descent, and they looked mean. Some were very overweight, of large build, with bushy beards and big bellies. They were filthy and smelled terrible. I shrank back when I saw the sheer number and size of them and wondered how I was going to survive. I looked wildly around me for some escape, but of course there was none. I called to my Angels, begged for help, then retreated to a sanctuary in my mind.

On the nights when gang members were off their faces on alcohol and drugs, their inhibitions were freed. I tried to protect myself by sometimes avoiding eye contact. I figured if I couldn't see them, then they couldn't really see me which meant I wasn't really there at all—it made sense to me, anyway. After a while, I stopped looking at them altogether and completely shut my eyes, but to some of them, this was offensive. The next thing I knew, I was being slapped or punched and yelled at to 'open your eyes, bitch'. This torture could go on for several days and nights. The Monster was never present, nor was he permitted to be. His job was to drive me there, take me to the gang leader and leave me there for the prearranged time. Sometimes it was overnight, sometimes for much longer.

One night, the situation got particularly out of hand and I was so badly beaten that I was unconscious when he came to collect me. I don't know exactly why they nearly killed me that night, but they did. My face was so smashed in that I was unrecognisable. Even The Monster was shocked. He said to the leader, 'You need to be careful about what you do to her because she won't look as good for you.' There was no inkling of concern for me whatsoever, no more than the worry that a key client of his might be disappointed if I didn't look as pretty for him the next time. The only concern was the potential loss of revenue if I was rejected as an 'ugly fucking bitch', as he called me when he took me to his mother's house to fix me up. He was furious, not with them, but with me. Clearly, I must have done something to deserve it.

I was weak, exhausted and in so much pain that I fell asleep with my last conscious thought being, why does he hate me so much?

I remember waking up in bed many hours or days later, terrified that I had worms crawling out of my skin. Whatever hallucinogenic drug they had given me was pretty strong and I couldn't remember much of what had happened. I couldn't tell anyone, and who cared anyway? The Monster certainly didn't. So, I just sat there and watched them crawl out of my skin and wondered how I could end my miserable life.

I don't know how long I stayed at Nana B's house to recover, but it felt like weeks. My nose had been broken, my face was swollen with bruising and I was struggling to breathe. Once again, the doctor had been called in—the same one who attended the abortion attempt. I now recognised his voice, as he was an existing 'Gentleman's Club' member. After he examined me, he looked shocked and said, 'She's been beaten really badly. She should be in hospital.' Of course, that would raise questions and they weren't going to risk that. Suffice to say, medication was supplied, instructions were given and I heard him say, 'Don't put her to work for a few weeks.' I was thrilled, and if I could have smiled without it hurting so much, I would have.

The Monster was angry, as it meant he wouldn't earn as much. He stormed out, yelling over his shoulder, 'As soon as she looks halfway decent, phone me. We need to get her back out there.'

Before too long, I was back working, which again included the gang. On some weekends and special events throughout that year, I was the main act. I can recall many things that made me physically sick, but I also recall an act of kindness. Unbelievable as it sounds, someone tried to help me.

On this occasion, I had been chained up outside to a tree beside a metal container full of beer. When gang members wanted a beer, they would come out there. They could do anything they liked to me and grab a beer at the same time. Most took advantage of the situation. I was given no food, water, or shelter; I just stayed chained up by that beer container for over two days.

During my second night there, a woman probably in her mid-thirties waited until the celebration inside was underway, then came out with a bowl and a cloth and cleaned up my face and body, held me close and told me I was going to be okay. She gave me some water to drink. She left and later checked on me throughout that night. She was the Angel I had been longing for who helped me survive through the pain and degradation I was put through. By doing that, she was risking her own safety, even her life, but her compassion won out and she still chose to help me. People have asked me in the years since why she didn't do more, but I was just grateful she even did that much. It was the only kindness I ever experienced within the gang walls and it gave me hope and the will to continue when I wanted to die. Consequently, whenever I heard the words 'Angels exist on earth', I used to think of her.

After a couple of weeks, I was taken home to my mother who never asked why I had been away from home for so long. Apparently, my grandmother had phoned her to say that I had asked to stay with her for a while and that she would get me to school during that time. My mother never questioned it, nor did she question why I was so thin, or looked so shaken. I was so relieved to see her, just wanted her to hold me in her arms and tell me it would all be okay, but her disinterest and low tolerance of me were firmly in charge. Life carried on and although I was still feeling weak and vulnerable, I put all that to one side, fell into line and carried on being the good Catholic daughter who 'honoured thy father and mother'.

I was living a double life and I had to survive. I just had to. In a way, my mother's disregard for me fuelled me to do well at school and elsewhere. Some part of me was looking for recognition, appreciation, or validation—something that would get her to finally 'see me'. Paradoxically, I have her to thank for never giving up, as in my quest for acceptance I strove harder, worked longer and pushed more than was typical of someone my age. I still had my friends, my sport and my part-time job.

After I turned fifteen, I started dating, which was a thrill for me. Back then, the only ways to meet others were through groups and church events and that's how I met Rob, at our local youth group where my best friend, Janet, and I went. As Rob was mates with Janet's boyfriend, Ant, we double-dated. Since they lived nearby, I would sometimes see them while staying at my father's house. He allowed it and in fact encouraged me to see my friends whilst staying with him. This was surprising until I realised why—it suited his purposes. The clock was ticking. I was getting older and would be turning sixteen within the year. He needed me to continue seeing him after that but knew legally I wasn't obliged to. That had been his agreement with my mother when the marriage ended. If I stopped going, his money stream ended. He couldn't pimp me out if I didn't choose to be there. The prospect was one he could not tolerate, but he wouldn't be able to force me, as my sixteenth birthday and therefore my liberation, were fast approaching.

He knew it, and so did I.

While Janet and the boys were welcome at my father's house, I never wanted them there. It was awful, had terrible associations for me, alongside being a filthy environment. On top of this, I felt shame at ever being in that 'house of horror'. Most of my free time was usually spent at Janet's. We would spend hours practising doing our hair and makeup so that we looked our best for the guys. We played records and spent time in her lounge practising dancing for hours and hours, secretly hoping our favourite songs would be played at whatever party we were going to that night, so we could magically get up and show everyone how talented we were.

There were times when I felt almost happy as we got ready for those dates. Janet's mother could sew very well and would make her lovely dresses to wear out. Although happy for her, I was also quite jealous and used to wish her mum was my real mother. She was also an accomplished baker and cook and would bake lovely biscuits and cakes for me to enjoy alongside the whole family. I remember thinking that if only I lived with them, I could eat like this every day. In fact, I used to avidly study her every move so I could learn to do things just as well when I had my own place.

Part of my recurring thought pattern growing up was wishing I were either someone else or that someone else's parents would adopt me. I think it was a fantasy of mine for as long as I could remember. As a teenager, I wasn't equipped to come to terms with why my parents didn't love me or want me. All I thought was perhaps I was better off without them, but until I was old enough to leave home, I had no choice. I was as stuck with them as they were with me. Well, in my mother's case anyway. She was tolerant of having my friends at home, but really just not that interested, so I never invited them in that much. She was happy for me to spend time with them, as it meant I was occupied, she just didn't want to invest in anything I was doing.

One of the benefits of going out with Rob was that he owned a car. We could all pile into it, head to the beach for the day, or go and visit friends. It was fun and, though not the love story of the year, we did manage to have a few laughs while we were dating, something that had been largely missing in my life for so long. Janet was someone I could confide in about Rob, about school and about everything to do with being a teenage girl. We used to lie out in the sun, cover ourselves with baby oil and try to get tanned in time for the next party.

What I never shared with Janet, though, was what it was like to live with The Monster—that was somewhere I would never go. Needless to say, she never stayed with me in his house as I couldn't handle a repeat of what happened with Michelle when I was twelve. In actual fact, I never told anyone at all. I think by then I had given up trying to tell people about what my life was really like. My reality was that no one cared or wanted to help anyway. I know being dissociated during the abuse was a factor, alongside fear. Fear of death, fear of my sisters being hurt and fear of him hurting other children. There was no way I was going to put my life at risk by speaking up and, as it was, I had become a master of suppression. Those threats made by The Monster were all too real. He had proven more than once that he would hurt me very badly if I was not entirely malleable whenever I was with him. I had been subconsciously conditioned for nearly sixteen years of my life. He had done his job well. I knew what actual threats and real danger looked like. So, I firmly blocked all the time I spent with him and I did such a great job—I didn't unblock those memories until sixteen years later.

Even while I was dating Rob, my services continued to be sold to various people and The Monster still had me entertaining friends and working out of various places, but his violence towards me was not as pronounced and he was not quite so fast to beat the shit out of me as was his wont in previous years. I thought things were going well and was starting to feel almost comfortable, until the night everything changed.

Rob and I had been at a friend's BBQ and had a few sneaky drinks. We left there and ended up parking up for some quiet kissing and cuddling nearby. When Rob dropped me off some time later, The Monster came to the door, shared a joke with him and ushered me inside. Once the door was closed, he started kicking and punching me, called me a 'dirty slut' then ripped off my clothes and violently raped me. He was uttering obscenities continually and asking if I 'enjoyed fucking Rob', saying that I was just a 'filthy whore' and that's all I would ever be.

When he had finished, he told me to stay where I was. He walked into the lounge and returned with a beer bottle. In those days, beer bottles were large and brown. He smacked me in the head, grabbed my legs and told me to roll over. I was then viciously sodomised with the bottle while he called me a 'dirty bitch', told me I 'wasn't worth shit' and that by the time he finished with me no one would ever want me again. I was bleeding profusely, shaking and crying and kept whispering, 'I'm sorry, I'm sorry, I'm sorry,' until I passed out with the pain.

When I woke sometime later, he had gone to bed. I managed to crawl down the long hallway in excruciating pain to my own bedroom, shaking and sore. I couldn't pull myself into bed, so I cried myself to sleep on the floor, wishing I was dead. The next day I couldn't walk. I was covered in bruises and still in agony. Rob and Janet turned up and I was made to hide. The Monster told them I wasn't there as even he knew the bruises would be a dead giveaway. I was then forced to stay with him for another few days till they faded and he could take me home.

BROTHEL

This chapter focuses on the brothel I worked in, specifically between twelve to sixteen years of age.

Back in the 1970s, there seemed to be a view that child prostitution, child slavery and child sex trafficking were not believed possible in New Zealand. The truth is, they were, and they happened in most cities across the country.

The brothel I worked out of was on K Road which is considered the red-light district in Auckland and frequented by people from all walks of life. Partygoers, couples just wanting to experiment, boys' nights out and so on. All seemingly good clean fun until you consider the misery lying behind it, including the extreme end of sexual deviancy where wads of cash changed hands. This is where my father, The Monster, could be found, counting his money and coming up with new definitions of evil.

I was to work out of there part-time for most of my teenage years. The first time I was taken there, The Monster parked the car and walked me in, where a rather large man greeted us. He ushered us into the club and told The Monster that The Boss would be in soon. We sat at the bar and I was riveted. Although the room was dark, there were coloured twinkling lights and loud music. The room was heavily decorated with maroon velvet and gold brocade. The stage was not large by today's standards, but big enough for four or more people to dance on at a time. Scantily clad, heavily made-up women paraded around. To me, they seemed very elegant. One of them came up, shucked me under by chin and gave The Monster a kiss on the cheek. He immediately grabbed her ass and made her sit on his lap.

Next thing, in walked The Boss. Not overly tall, balding and fat. I couldn't take my eyes off of his unbuttoned shirt and the gold chains hanging from his neck. As The Monster started discussing terms of trade, which involved leasing me from the brothel, The Boss asked what I could do. The Monster replied, 'She'll do whatever you want, no questions asked, but there are rates for special extras.' As they continued discussing what services I could provide, I was given pink lemonade by the bartender, a heavily made-up transgender woman called Lucy. She gave me a wink and a smile, then served the men their drinks. I was in awe—I loved the feathers and the dress she wore and wanted to be just like her.

After a few more minutes of discussion, The Boss wanted to see what I could do so I was taken upstairs to do some performing for him. As he was molesting me The Monster looked on and barked commands of, 'Move your hips, moan loudly, shake your ass,' and so on. I did what he said, but The Boss was rough and big and wanted to rape me doggy style. I didn't like it. I tried to squirm away and that's when I got slapped across the back of the head. Not by The Monster, but by The Boss. That was my first inkling that this was more dangerous than I thought. I was instantly scared and realised if he would do that in front of The Monster, what would happen if he wasn't there? He continued until he had finished, then pulled me up by the hair and said, 'You'll do.' I started crying because he hurt me. The Monster came right up to my face and barked, 'Shut the fuck up, you should be grateful The Boss wants you here at all.'

He then told me to clean myself up and that he would be back to pick me up in the morning. When I dared to ask what he meant, he said, 'You're working here tonight, do what you're told. I'll see you tomorrow.' He left the room discussing the appeal of chaining me up for the punters.

I was by myself in that room for what seemed like forever, in a dream, until there was a knock at the door. A young woman named Rose came in, looked shocked and asked me how old I was. When I told her, she came and gave me a hug told me not to be too scared, that most of 'the Johns' were ok and wouldn't hurt me. She asked me if I was alright and said she could bring me free food and drinks if I wanted. I said I didn't think I was allowed to drink. She told me I wouldn't get through the night if I didn't. She disappeared and returned with a 'yummy' drink that made me feel a little silly and giggly. But she was right, I did feel a little better and a bit more relaxed. She was kind, and in between her clients and mine, she would come and check on me. I liked her and felt safer knowing she was there.

At some stage during the night, she brought in a couple of other women who worked at the club. They were clearly interested in me and the situation I was in and started asking lots of questions. I was too scared to say anything much, unsure of who I could trust. But I could tell, they were not happy to have me there. Not because I was any threat to their business, but because I was so young.

During the night, I wasn't allowed downstairs because then people would see me and notice how young I actually was, so I spent all night upstairs. The Boss came up regularly, not to check on me but to bring me my next 'John'. Rose was right, most of them were okay and didn't deliberately try to hurt me too much. The only problem being, they knew what sexual acts they were paying for and I hadn't been told, so it was a struggle for me. I didn't understand what was coming next and I just wanted to go home.

So began my first night of working on K Road as a child prostitute.

The only differences between the real sex workers and I were that I was twelve, I was frightened and I wanted my mummy.

Interestingly, after that initial weekend, I didn't mind going there. Of all the groups and places my father trafficked me to, K Road was the nicest for me. I got used to the work and the men and became familiar with what was expected. The main reason though was that I quite enjoyed getting to know the others who worked there. Partly because they looked out for me and were kind to me; partly because I got free food and drinks. Another plus was that The Monster was not there scrutinising my every move, which meant on those days I wasn't beaten or kicked or threatened. For the most part he was just the driver, though at times he would come in and hang out with The Boss.

During the afternoons if neither he nor The Boss were there, Lucy or one of the others would give me money to go and buy an ice cream. I loved that part, having a treat without The Monster knowing was a rarity. Underneath it all, I was a bit anxious that someone would tell him and I would be in trouble. But they all assured me that no one would. I discovered over time that no one actually liked The Monster. I could tell because they didn't want to talk to him when he came in, or they would walk away and make some excuse. They had noticed how he spoke to me and treated me, had seen the bruises. But they had also noticed his smarmy pseudo-charm and how it was all an act to get either sex or money. I heard them talking about him one day and words like 'fake', 'bastard' and 'slimy' were all used. This brought a smile to my face and gave me more confidence around them, as the minute he was gone, they were safe to be kind and gentle towards me. I realised I felt something I never had before, I felt liked. As I never normally experienced this, it vindicated me in a way. If they liked me, maybe I wasn't so unlovable after all. Maybe people could see some good in me?

The Monster had told me I was privileged to work at the club as the men who requested me were 'very, very important' and I should be grateful. He told me I had been chosen to service them and provide comfort for them. I should show my thanks as I was very lucky and therefore, I had better make it special for them. That was code for allowing them to do whatever they liked, however they liked. The alternative was getting the shit kicked out of me, starved and left for days.

My brothel experience went on for years and the routine became familiar. If he picked me up from my mother's house, a stop-off at the club would be made. In the end, my so-called weekend access visits to my father became my main sex slavery and trafficking days. I grew to hate him more and more.

While all this was happening, my mother remarried. His name was Bob. I was fifteen at the time and thought he seemed okay, not overly interested in me, which was a bonus in my opinion, nor was he overly opinionated. Double bonus. I had dreamed that when my mother remarried, I would finally have a good father figure in my life. That was not to be, as although Bob wasn't aggressive in nature, he was a raging alcoholic whose first and foremost love was whiskey. Once he started drinking, his behaviour became predatory. Once again, I was in danger, at home, with nowhere to go. I had so wanted to feel, what my mother kept repeating over and over again, that 'Bob was a good man.'

She had been introduced to him by her brother-in-law who worked alongside Bob as an electrical engineer in Pakuranga. They had dated for several months when the decision was made to marry and relocate the family to Pakuranga so Bob could be close to his work. Never mind that the rest of us had to travel for hours each day to get to school and work, it suited both my mother and him for us to sell up and move out.

Initially, I had no inkling that there was anything untoward about Bob, rather he seemed very quiet and introverted, which was a relief. I felt awkward around him, but not overly fussed and was feeling quite excited about moving and having my own room for the first time in years.

I think the first time I realised he was not quite the 'good man' my mother wanted me to believe he was, was when he preyed on me at their wedding. Out of sight of the wedding guests, he tried to kiss me passionately on the mouth. I was shocked and frightened. I looked around for someone to help me, but it was the usual suspects: my family and extended family members who had been complicit in the abuse my entire life. I felt I had no choice, but to run from the venue at 11 pm at night and although I didn't feel safe on the streets, it was safer for me than staying at the wedding.

I never told Mum. I knew there was no point. She had never believed a word I had said throughout my life, why would she start now? On one occasion over the next few years, I tried to broach the subject with her, of Bob touching me inappropriately, but she told me not to be ridiculous and that he was just being friendly. That was it for me; I never again went to her with anything about my abuse until I was in my thirties.

It was a confusing time for me, because when he wasn't drunk, making suggestive comments or touching me inappropriately, he was actually kind to me. I wasn't used to that and didn't know how to process it. What was even more confusing was his generosity—he would teach me to drive or drop me at my friends or ask about my day. In some ways that was harder to bear because he wasn't angry and violent towards me, so I felt I owed him. I was so confused and mixed up, I didn't know how to react.

My mother, of course, knew nothing or at least pretended not to. In retrospect, it seemed she loved the fact that Bob got on so well with me, as that meant she didn't have to give me any attention. In other words, he was doing her job. I can now see what a chronic enabler she was. She had now empowered both her husbands to abuse or take advantage of me at their whim. Though they sat on other ends of the personality scale, their behaviour towards me was still toxic and dysfunctional. What was extremely difficult to accept was knowing what was really going on. I just didn't have the words or comprehension to express it. I had never given up the long-held illusion that one day she would magically look after me and love me.

Again, I was wrong.

One of my recurring fantasies was that my mother's remarriage and relocation meant The Monster's access to me would stop. I liked to believe the distance was too great, so it would make pick-ups and drop-offs prohibitively time-consuming. In actuality, the opposite was true. Not only did he have access, but it became for longer periods because it was 'too far' for my mother to come and pick me up. That usually entailed Bob offering to do it, which meant I had not one but two fathers vying for the opportunity to abuse me. Needless to say, I was starting to feel enslaved wherever I was.

My new life with Bob carried on as another scene in the nightmare of my adolescence. The brothel narrative continued and every second weekend, I was required to perform. Although sex was the biggest commodity sold, pornographic movies also commanded a good audience and therefore a high money return. I was to star in many of these movies over the years, from when I was just three years old right up until I was sixteen. The earlier footage was taken in a downstairs room at someone's house in West Auckland and during the later years, the film set was upgraded to K Road. In total, I would feature in up to a hundred of these movies made and then distributed to the highest bidder.

One memory I have of being filmed was being given a lovely silky fabric to drape over my body and being fussed over with my hair. In order to make me fully relax, I was given a sickly spiked orange drink. I noticed, peeking out from behind the curtains, that there was a shiny projector and a whirring film reel. To me, it looked expensive and the man standing behind it seemed professional.

I had been told that I was very lucky to have been chosen to feature in the movies and that not many children had this opportunity. If I did well, I was promised more treats and fun than I could ever imagine. I just had to do what I was told and I might even get to go horse riding!

There were several men in the room and a couple of women. The women were mainly there to ensure I looked okay and that costumes stayed on and in place. Eventually though they would become part of the movie itself.

The room itself had a couple of poles in it and was the largest room there. Someone put on a record, a man with a beard told me what to do and then it was 'lights, camera, action!' I had to dance around the stage and just enjoy myself. This was fun, I thought, I loved dancing. That progressed, however, into sexy dancing. Cries of 'move your hips', 'smile more' and 'bend over' were called out to me. I was feeling uncomfortable about this as I wasn't wearing underwear and was only covered by silky material.

As the director barked further instructions, the sexualisation became more explicit and felt more and more shameful and embarrassing. Within a few minutes, they called for another girl to come on stage. We had to touch each other, gyrating and calling out that we wanted more. It was dreadful and I just wanted to run.

After a few hours of this, we were given a short break and allowed to go buy an ice cream. This was a big deal, as it was tiring, embarrassing and hot in there. The second part of the filming was so much worse that it made the morning seem like a teddy bears' picnic. We were required to begin performing oral sex. The drugs we were given helped to block some, but not all of it out. It then went a step further with us being required to insert objects into each other while looking sexily and with lust into the camera. We were hurting each other and struggling. The director and The Monster were not happy. At one stage I heard the director ask him if he thought I was ready for this. 'She's ready for anything,' The Monster said, 'I've trained her well.' Filming took all day and by the end we were utterly exhausted and miserable. I know the other girl was struggling just as I was and we both started to cry. But although she got to go home once the filming was finished, I was then sold to a few paedophiles to make The Monster feel like he had had a worthwhile and productive day.

The next film shoot was a few months later. This time the stakes were higher and it wasn't just children and objects that were involved. For this particular shoot, we had men sitting around that we had to perform on and for. In no set order: oral sex, sodomy, rape and, of course, objects. The more fantastical the scene, the more money they could apparently make. Once again, with us drugged, dressed for action, bribed with treats and horses, the camera rolled.

Once again, no treats were ever given.

Because of the sexual abuse I endured from such a young age, my body was used to being invaded and hurt, but sometimes it was just too much for me physically. Whether as a predictor of that or just out of plain common sense, my grandmother had made a salve to apply to my nether regions before going to the nightclub and doing the filming. This was a lifesaver as I was abused so much during that time that I felt like I was on fire. Whatever was in there offered some relief, but I do know herbs from my Aunty Iris' garden were part of the concoction used. Although I had nothing to be grateful to her about, that was one thing that helped with the inflammation and pain prolonged and repeated rape had on me.

I used to apply it feverishly, hoping it would numb me. That wasn't the case, but it did go a long way to keeping me functioning and out of hospital.

As the months wore on, so did the filming at the nightclub. I became adept at recognising what would get me through in the least painful way. I used my chameleon skills to get kindness as opposed to violence from anyone I could. I had figured out if I could appeal to the men's vanity, they would be kinder and gentler with me. I was worried about being hurt and I was frightened. I often felt as though I would crumple before going on stage and I hated that. I made it my mission to protect myself as much as I could, so that I could get through it all as easily as possible. I would sidle up to a gentler-looking participant and ask what he liked the most. I would promise he would get what he liked if he would be kind to me. This was hit and miss in its appeal.

Sometimes it worked.

Sometimes it didn't.

GENTLEMEN'S CLUB

Although the following experiences occurred throughout most of my childhood, the events described in this chapter focus on those between the ages of twelve to sixteen.

Some of my abusers belonged to the club The Monster was a member of. I first met a handful of them in my grandmother's front parlour when I was six and would unknowingly inhabit their world for the next ten years.

I didn't know who they were until I was older, all I knew was that they were very important and commanded respect. They wore dark suits and drove flash cars. One was of political renown because he had a driver and a bodyguard. The other esteemed clientele included High Court judges, top policemen and various influential members of the upper echelons of society. I know this because I overheard The Monster bragging to my grandmother about them.

These paedophiles were evil, backed by money, prestige and power. They formed part of a secret society which orchestrated a large-scale global child pornography and paedophile ring. I'm not sure how powerful the current link is between them and other paedophile rings in New Zealand today, but it was strong back then. There were many children besides me who suffered at their hands and this continued unabated, and will continue to do so, until they are fully exposed for who they are and what they do.

It did not appear that every person who belonged to the club was a child abuser. Perhaps they were not high enough up the chain to have access to the paedophile ring, but by association they were tainted by this group. The criminal and legal powers behind them were incredibly powerful and far-reaching. The Monster became quite an influential member of this club, simply because of the currency he provided through his child sex slave. Namely me.

There were many events over the years and copious occasions on which I would be requested to perform for them, and specifically for the person in charge. Being aware of this, I knew it wasn't worth risking my life by being anything other than reverential and grateful. I was almost expecting a man wearing a crown with an incredible aura and benevolence. Instead, what I got was a flabby old man with body odour and untrimmed nose hair.

The club had many satellites throughout New Zealand and overseas, as well as having outposts in outlying rural areas. It was to the latter places that many of us were taken to be abused. Often if there was a celebration of some kind, other chapters would turn up to celebrate as well. It was at these occasions that a medical unit would be made available so that all of the children could be drugged and checked over for injuries or infections, both before and after these events. Most commonly though, during the proceedings something would occur which would require medical intervention as well.

The remote venues would be chosen for their privacy and distance from other dwellings. It was also standard practise for them to be heavily guarded by police. Black and white police cars flanked the entrance to the rather long driveways, but I don't know if they were aware of the criminal activity that occurred within the grounds or not.

The problem, as far as I was concerned, was that if they did know, how could I trust them enough to tell them anything? It didn't take long for the answer to hit me squarely in the face. I couldn't.

Once again, I had not one safe adult I could talk to or take this to—a recurring theme throughout my childhood and adolescence. Even if an adult might have had concerns, it would have only taken my parents' charm and flattery to change their minds.

Although the club had a network throughout the country, The Monster belonged to one in particular. It was there I would regularly go each month. During their meetings, they would wear masks so as to be unrecognisable, but they couldn't disguise their voices, so over time I began to recognise my abusers when they spoke.

There was a hierarchy that existed within the club and membership was through invitation only. It seemed the higher up you were, the more power you had, and this worked very well for The Monster. He quickly learned how and what to provide for them, as this ensured him more kudos and notoriety as he quickly scaled their ranks. But the truth was, it was only because he could provide them with a 'trained' and 'willing' child to abuse. This is what stood him in good stead and gave him the recognition and power he so patently craved. As time went by, he was required to provide more and more favours to them, which translated to me being forced into the kind of depravity no one believes exists.

Satanic abuse.

For most humans, their innate moral compass and conscience would stop such evil and cruelty being inflicted upon children and animals.

It goes against everything that is morally acceptable. However, it did happen, and I believe it still does.

This group had a ritualistic approach to their abuse. Everything was done within a strict order and conducted precisely.

Those of us that were to be brought into their rooms were first taken into a separate area and stripped naked. We were made to line up and be tended to by the doctor and his nurse. This usually meant being forced to lie on the table while a needle was jabbed into our arms. I later recognised this as some sort of barbiturate, which rendered us dissociative and malleable. Once the drug had taken effect, the nurse would check us over, and when we had the all-clear, we were taken into another room and laid out in a circle to allow the men to abuse us more easily.

As the men walked in, there was a protocol to follow. The leader would have first pick and thereby secure his place in the circle. He would start chanting softly at first, growing louder and louder. The next man would take his place beside him and so on until all places were filled. The chanting would get louder and louder as ritualistic sexual abuse ensued. There would be up to eighteen men at a time in that room. After a bell was rung, another chant would begin. Once they had finished with a child, they would stand by and wait for the sign to start on the next. The nurse would come around and wipe up the children whilst keeping her gaze averted. She never made eye contact with either the men or any of us. The ritualism made it sicker than anything I had experienced up until this point.

During these events, the men were high and were encouraged to express themselves however they wished. While they were very excited and ready for action, the opposite was true for us kids.

Often, I would hear the younger children crying or calling out for their mummies. Being one of the older ones, I tried to comfort them as much as I could. But whatever I did, I knew I couldn't stop what was going to happen to them. I felt protective towards them, and it was a very real dilemma because I knew they were frightened and didn't understand what was happening to them. One small boy named Leon concerned me greatly. He would have only been five years old and he couldn't stop whimpering. I knew some of the men were starting to notice and, should he carry on, they would punish him further.

When their backs were turned, I encouraged Leon to think about his favourite cartoon and hum the tune for me. As I was able to distract him enough to stop him whimpering, the attention went elsewhere. Our abuse and torture continued on and on until the men had had enough. Sometimes it wasn't full rape or sodomy, sometimes it could just be hands. Other times, they would turn us around so they could force their penises into our mouths. Whatever it was, it went on through the night.

There were other events held within their club throughout those years. One involved slitting animals' throats and forcing us to drink their blood or smearing it on our bodies. They usually involved the leader offering the animal to signify a particular occasion or mark a specific event. These ritualistic acts were bizarre, with no warning about what would happen next, and traumatic to experience.

May Day, the first day of May, was a major celebration for this group. Candles and incense would be lit, followed by chanting and singing, with the celebrations lasting for hours. Long speeches were given and toasts made, all while we children were expected to lie there and wait.

One night, towards the end of the proceedings, there was even mention of human sacrifice. I froze, because I understood clearly that The Monster would not hesitate to offer me up if it would elevate his standing in the club. However, my Angels were standing guard that night, as for some reason he didn't leap at the chance. It wasn't until the next day that I overheard him telling someone that if I were dead, his revenue would be cut, which meant he would be back to doing more of the menial work he hated and he wasn't about to let that happen. Even though I was so miserable, part of me was relieved I wouldn't be sacrificed—I was worth too much to him alive. The nightmare of this incident visited me every time I was dragged to the club, but it wasn't long until my sixteenth birthday and freedom from my father. This was what kept me going, that realisation, and my Angels. I would talk to them all the time and feel their love and guidance. And although that sounds unusual for a fifteen-year-old, they were all I had. They stood by me and kept me going when no one else would.

During that year, I was working at Farmers department store in Pakuranga on weekends and during holiday periods. I enjoyed the money I earned, and I especially liked the Christmas season because I was rostered on for more shifts, which kept me away from home. The boss seemed nice and the staff were friendly. It was a safe place and I could spend my money how I liked.

At home, life carried on much as it always had. By this time Debbie was seventeen, studying to be an electrical engineer and had joined a fundamentalist church group, where she spent all of her spare time.

This seemed to fill a need in her and she was often at their events over the weekends. Christine, at twenty-one, had long left home and was working as a flight attendant. She had worked hard for what she got and was eventually able to buy her own home. I always saw her as glamorous and used to envy her lifestyle. She bought beautiful artefacts back from countries she had been to and seemed to be 'living the dream'. I wasn't overly close to either sister as I was so dissociated and cut off from the real me that I couldn't possibly connect in any meaningful way with another person. Out of the two though, I felt more of a connection to Debbie as she was softer in nature and closer in age. Unfortunately, we didn't really have anything in common, as I was either working, being trafficked by The Monster, or out with my friends.

I was in my sixth form year at school and was studying hard to pass my exams, which in those days was called University Entrance. Sometimes I would get up at four in the morning to study so I would still have time to work that day or get to school. My friends were busy with their lives, but we did used to hang out on the weekends when we could. It was an interesting time, as my mother was becoming more well-known and writing many self-help books on topics like, stress, marital advice and confidence-building. She had also started running seminars for people and was often on radio talking about various topics. She was quite well known at the time and she adored all the attention. Her marriage to Bob continued to be encapsulated by him drinking himself into a stupor most nights and her pretending everything was fine. This usually took the form of her watching TV in the lounge, while he would be in the garage tinkering and drinking like a fish. To say this was a happy functioning household was patently untrue. It just wasn't. It was also version number two of her first marriage: pretending everything was fine while the underbelly patiently slithered nearby.

My relationship with my mother had deteriorated so much that I tried to detach as much as I could. I just didn't want to be around her. Although I didn't understand it at the time, I was rejecting her. She had created the scenario where her falseness and narcissism meant she didn't have room for me in her life, so I eventually got the message and, although I was living with her, I carried on my life independently. I had to find my way as I had unconsciously been doing since I was born. Now I was older, I started doing it consciously. Interestingly she never noticed. She had never 'seen me' so I shouldn't have been surprised. What she never got was that once my dependency on her grew less so did my respect and faith in her. I had always yearned for her love, had always felt bereft without it. That hadn't changed, but what had, was the dawning realisation that I would be okay without her and, as I was becoming older, I was separating away from her more and more. Though that is typical of teenagers, this was much more damaging, as I wasn't a typical teenager and she wasn't a typical mother.

However, I still did what she wanted, I still fit 'the carer' role, but I was less inclined to be with her and just went through the motions. Bob, in his pissed state, was not a person to be cognisant of anything, let alone recognising that the relationship between his wife and her youngest was damaged beyond repair. I was still considered 'the black sheep' and though I played my part admirably, there was a very damaged and disintegrated girl underneath it all. I couldn't connect with anyone in my family. I felt cast adrift, alone at sea, never knowing when the next tsunami would hit.

I began hanging out with my neighbour and her friends. She was a lot older than me and her husband had died. I used to look after her young boys while she went out and loved the fact I wasn't at home in my mother's house with her disinterest and Bob. My mother, of course, was thrilled, as the further out of her sight I was, the easier it was for her to pretend I didn't exist, and as that suited us both, it seemed to work. However, this was to change as something else was coming down the pipeline, totally unexpected and yet bizarrely welcome.

I got glandular fever, out of the blue, and just like that it meant I was bedridden for months. I don't know how closely involved my Angels were in this, but I do know this helped me enormously. I was too ill to go to my father's house. This was the second miracle for me and one I couldn't have been more grateful for. To have the respite, to not have to be subjected to the abuse, trafficking, prostitution, movies and bestiality was such a gift. I didn't really have conscious thoughts of this at the time, I was just grateful I could stay put, albeit in my mother's house.

I was very ill and needed medical attention—quite a lot initially. Even though my mother had largely ignored me, even she couldn't ignore that. I looked terrible, had become more emaciated and was exhausted. For several months over that year, I was bedridden. I couldn't sit my exams at the end of the year, which meant I failed to get my University Entrance qualification. I was miserable as I'd worked so hard to do well at school, but there was nothing to be done. I had to accept it and carry on.

I didn't see people at that time, as I spent most of my time just sleeping. I had a visit from one friend at school and Janet and Ant turned up sometimes, but really, I was too sick to see anyone. My family had no choice but to look after me and my mother even took me to see a specialist. She was concerned, well, as much as she could be, but really it was left to Bob to bring in food and drinks for me. He did so and seemed genuinely worried. Surprisingly, it was during those months I felt the safest with him I ever had. It was weird in a way as although he was a predator when drunk, when I was this unwell he was kind and quite alarmed by the sight of me. It was he rather than my mother who would check in on me and make sure I was okay. Although my mother was worried, I knew her kindness and concern would dissipate, as she was much too important to play the nurse for long. Sure enough, after several days, she went back to being the classic narcissist she was.

I never saw my father during those months. He did ring to try and persuade me to come and 'recover' at his place, but I was too sick and didn't want to see him again anyway. At no time did he come around to check on me, or to enquire as to how I was, understandable as if I couldn't earn for him, why would he bother? I was just relieved he didn't. Being free from torture meant so much to me. When I reflect on those months, I wonder if being that ill was a culmination of all the suffering and trauma I had undergone over the preceding years.

I can't help but think it was.

THE MAGICAL 16

For most of my life, the numbers 1 and 6 have always held a special meaning. Whenever I got a car park with the numbers 1, 6 or 16, I took it as a sign. If a café table displayed any of those numbers, I was secretly delighted. In fact, anywhere 1 and 6 popped up, I felt reassured. I would actively look for them wherever I went, not understanding why they meant so much. When it finally clicked, it was obvious: From my sixteenth birthday, I never had to see The Monster again.

Right from the day my parents separated, the agreement had always been that he would have legal access to me until I turned sixteen. This meant every second weekend and half of school holidays. I was not allowed a say in this, rather I was forced to go until the day of that magical birthday. June 1976 stands out as the most incredible time of my life up until that point, simply because, for the first time, I could choose whether or not to see The Monster ever again. I was quite different from the naive eleven-year-old who had been tricked into living with him. I had grown up, and this time I knew what my answer would be, had known it for years. No, I would not choose to see him. I never wanted to see him again and nothing would change my mind.

The difficulty, of course, was my mother, who tried to tell me that he loved me and that he just didn't know how to show it. That was, of course, easier for her, as she had chosen years earlier to avoid any communication, let alone confrontation, with him. But I knew enough by then to realise I was lucky to be alive and should I endure more visits with him that luck may not continue.

The biggest hurdle was telling him, as my mother again required me to do this alone and unsupported rather than taking responsibility for this herself as she should have. In other words, she offered no assistance whatsoever. My mother had made it clear she would never willingly speak to my father unless she was forced to do so. Her agenda was to avoid him at all costs, regardless of the fact that I needed her support when dealing with him. She had never showed any willingness to stand alongside me before, but I still held a fervent hope that she would. As the day to my birthday drew near, she was to prove once again that I couldn't rely on her. Once again, I was left alone and scared in managing this momentous decision in my life.

On my birthday when he phoned, I was naturally terrified at what his reaction would be. He was initially smarmy and pleasant; wished me happy birthday and said he would like to take me out. I started shaking and had to sit down. I nearly said 'yes', but I wasn't going to be sucked in, so I took a deep breath and said 'no'.

After a stunned silence, he demanded to know why not. I made up some excuse. He said something along the lines of, 'Your loss, don't expect a present then.' As he went on to say he would pick me up on Friday after school, I took a deep breath, as the world spun on its axis in anticipation, and said I didn't want to come and stay with him anymore. He was shocked, became whiny and then angry and demanded to speak to my mother. I was expecting all of that as that was how he operated. She took the call, listened for a minute then looked angrily at me. She told him to hold on a minute, covered the mouthpiece and told me not to be so selfish and that I should see him, he was my father. I was knocked back by that, but I was determined not to be hurt anymore, so I stood my ground and kept saying 'no'.

She gave the phone back to me without saying a word to either of us then stalked off. When I said hello, he began to manipulate me, and my bravery waned. It was not only challenging, but terrifying. I had never stood up to this man before and he was not taking it well.

This was a person who had manipulated and tortured me all of my life and I knew he had all sorts of hell to unleash on me if he could. Nonetheless I was strong in my refusal and kept saying 'no'. After a few long silences he realised I wasn't going to change my mind. Eventually following an interminable silence, he said to me, 'You will regret this.'

That marked the end of the life I had lived till then, and the beginning of feeling bone-shattering relief. I was free and filled with joy, released from knowing that I could no longer be forced to have anything to do with him. I wholeheartedly believed life could really become something wonderful from then on, and felt I at least deserved that.

I should have known better.

My father, cruel as he was, was not known to take 'no' as an answer. Over the next few months, he persisted with phone calls, invitations to events and activities he knew I would love, even bribing me with the promise of a car if I would go and spend time with him. Thankfully, I was much wiser and older and maintained my refusal. While I had breath in my body, I was never going back there. Ever. I don't know how I found the courage to do so, as he had wielded such power over me, throughout my life, but I did. I kept saying 'no'.

From then on, though I never willingly chose to see my father again, there were times over the ensuing years where he would attend a family funeral or wedding. Inevitable though it was, I would always feel a sense of dread that I would see him in the distance, so I tried to avoid him as much as possible.

Though it would appear simple and straightforward, the shift from 'having to go' to 'not having to go' would prove anything but. My joy at being 'free' was only in part, as I still needed to live under my mother's roof and be subjected to Bob. Although still gentle in nature, he continued his sexualised behaviour towards me and my ongoing challenge was to traverse the sense of disconnect I felt living with him, whilst at the same time adapting to the post-traumatic stress I suffered daily.

I hadn't considered, let alone processed, that life was going to be an ongoing monumental challenge. I had sustained so much psychological harm that I was fragmented and disintegrating. It would take many decades of healing before I could possibly hope to undo or even attempt to undo the harm that was done. My experience had imprinted on me that trust, kindness and goodness were not available to someone like me. Neither men nor women could be trusted, a lesson I had learnt well.

A question I have been asked many times and which I have researched myself is why I didn't tell anyone—friends, safe adults, police what was happening to me. As with everything in my life, the answer is shrouded in layer upon layer of complexity. Perhaps the most compelling reason was conditioning. Being designated from birth as a sex slave, one fit for purpose, meant I wasn't afforded a real identity.

My perception of myself was that I did not matter and held no value. As I wasn't valued by others, finding my own sense of self-worth to the point where I would finally proclaim the truth or seek help was unlikely.

From that premise, it would have been out of character to be rescued by someone who gave a damn when I didn't give one for myself. Alongside that, because of the daily nature of the abuse, I got used to it as a normal part of my life, almost as familiar and mundane as brushing my teeth. Given the recurring onslaught, it made no difference whether it was physical, verbal or sexual. The challenge I faced around my abusers was in trying to become invisible and quiet so as to not call attention to myself. It was almost as though what I underwent was normal, or so I thought. A secret was being kept, one I was complicit in, as well as being a victim of. At the beginning, I was too young and confused to ask for help. My parents were my caregivers and what they did and said was the law. As I got older, it was far too dangerous to even consider, but none of that changed one simple truth: on the inside I was screaming for help and for someone to rescue me.

A further reason I didn't disclose was that my parents acted so differently around people outside of our home, and, as children do, I copied what I saw. They behaved as if everything was fine and we were a happy normal family with no real concerns. I did what they did, partly because it was easier and partly because it was expected. Few words were explicitly spoken; it was more subtle and dangerous than that. Although I didn't really understand everything that was going on, I knew that around others I had to be silent. Perhaps the most difficult part was the deadly threats made against my sisters and mother. I believed everything my father said, having experienced his anger too many times not to. That alone ensured I would shut up and keep quiet.

Although during my childhood people would on occasion ask how I was, I couldn't trust them as I had been tricked and deceived so many times. I was too scared to take the risk that they might be genuine. In the end, there was only one acceptable answer: 'Fine, thank you.' I'm sure people wondered what was going on, or at the very least why my family was so dysfunctional, but back then no one would have considered doing anything about it.

Regardless, it was a hallmark of my absolute desperation that during those eighteen months living with my father that I proactively tried to get help. As mentioned earlier, I often ran up to the phone box to call the police, knowing they may not be trustworthy. I was desperate to be rescued but always too scared to talk, the dilemma being that I would have felt safer in their hands than in my father's.

I even planned my escape from home by hiding myself in his mates' cars so I could be driven away to safety. Upon discovering me, though shocked, they never seemed particularly concerned to know the reason a young girl would stow herself away in their car. As I always had my bag of clothes with me, it was obvious I was trying to escape but they wilfully turned a blind eye. These were my father's friends after all, so I shouldn't have been surprised. If they were at our house, they were either complicit in the abuse or had no interest in helping me.

To my childlike mind, anyone or anywhere else seemed a better and safer option for me. This was all I could think of doing to try and escape the torture my life with him was. They would phone my father, put me back in the car and return me to him. This was to be repeated several times over the period I spent living with him. The consequences and punishments for my crimes were dire, usually involving starvation, beatings, or worse. My behaviour became sadder and more desperate, culminating in multiple attempts to take my own life to bring an end to my misery once and for all. Nowadays, I would be hopeful that the crisis team or police would intervene, support would be given and I would be saved. Back then, no one got involved, so I was just left to it. No one wanted to know, so whatever they saw or thought they saw was always ignored.

Another at-risk behaviour I engaged in was sometimes walking for hours at night, alone on the streets. Again, though seen by many, I was never stopped and asked if I needed help. I tried as hard as I could to show people how distressed I was, but not a single person picked up what I was putting down, and so the cycle continued.

Once the eighteen months of hell were over and I was back with my mother, I became even more complicit in the cover-up. It was safer that way. My sisters never talked about the abuse, so there was no permission for me to 'talk' either. I just had to cope with it. Being just a teenager who had been systemically and repeatedly brainwashed to keep quiet about what was happening, I didn't know any different and this was expected. It became the only acceptable option in our family and community—keep it hidden, keep it quiet, sweep it all under the rug. These were the 60s and 70s, when society was not configured to recognise paedophilia, child trafficking or domestic violence the way it is now. There would have been shock and outrage, followed by a growing disbelief and concern around why a child would make it all up. Since the truth would have been too much to bear, it was easier to turn the child into an attention-seeking liar.

In that era, people did not seem to know of, or talk about, child prostitution or paedophiles. While the term 'child prostitute' causes outrage, I don't know what else to call what I was and did. I was a child who was sold or leased to perform sexual acts on adults, as well as performing in filming of these events. Although I have researched this, I cannot find a better term to describe it.

Back then, children had no rights. It was expected that parents would look after their families in a loving and protective way. It was the norm for families to be dictated to by the head of the household, and it was considered bad form to interfere in another man's family life.

In this environment, the conditions were perfect for the prolific and cruel abuse to grow and flourish. Ignorance, disinterest and gullibility all had their part to play in the permission given for this status quo to continue. These traits were embodied by the adults around me—family, extended family, school, church, neighbours and the list goes on. Where a blind eye was turned, or 'that's not our business' was touted, hell was encouraged to continue on its evil and unrelenting path.

It is children's behaviour, not their words, that reveals the truth. In the first few years in the school system, my behaviour caused great concern and anger, both there and at home. The problem was that I didn't put on a good front to the adults at school because I felt safe there. Feverishly seeking their attention, kindness, even food, was top of mind for me. In the presence of 'safe' adults and away from my parent's eyes, I was considered difficult and naughty. It seems I would do anything for attention, I was desperate you see, desperate for someone to rescue me. The worse I behaved, the more attention I got, and though it may have seemed counterproductive, getting negative attention was at least some attention. In a sheltered place like school,

I mattered. To have the feeling that I was seen and recognised for something by a 'safe' adult was a gift to me.

I feel sure that my Angels must have been working hard to ensure this happened, as even though the nuns would tear their hair out in frustration, I had won—a small part of me was seen. I was alive, I was a somebody, I wasn't a thing. This didn't translate to keeping me safe or removing me from the family home, the opposite was true. Their frustration with me would escalate to the point my parents would be called in, but it was quickly ascertained I was just naughty. It never got me anywhere, but a small spark was ignited: if I am seen, then I am someone, if I am someone, I must count.

Due to the Catholic Church and its doctrine, the nuns had no power to act even had they wanted to. These were selfless women who had given their lives to serve, but they were also powerless and not overly revered. That was put aside for the Catholic priests who were treated like God himself. A priest came to our home occasionally, but it was always just a social call and both parents made sure to impress him and dissuade him from any negative thoughts about their parenting skills, or lack thereof. Again, had this been a different era, more compelling questions may have been asked, but as it was, no one did, which just reconfirmed that no one cared.

In every way possible, I showed my pain and suffering, and though people must have suspected something was terribly wrong, there was never any serious follow up. There was no permission back then to be anything other than 'acceptable' so to have anyone want to know why I was sad or behaving badly was never really discussed.

Though there are layers upon layers to this. The only reason the abuse continued was due to the silence enabling it.

Another question I have been asked repeatedly, is how it is possible for me to have forgotten the events of those years once I was safe. Simply put, due to the prolonged and traumatic events throughout my childhood, my mind had protected me. It is well known that the mind has many ways of guarding against trauma and mine chose to repress all of those sixteen years of childhood memories. In other words, I blocked them out. While the beatings and rapes were happening to me, I would leave my body and go somewhere else in my mind. It was too hard, too traumatic and too painful to stay with the actual events occurring.

I have come to learn that this is not uncommon among adult survivors of child sexual abuse, but mine went way beyond that. Repressing the events of those years meant I could function and have as normal a life as possible within the circumstances of my home life. That meant I was able to live and survive in the everyday world. I could sit down and eat with the family having completely blocked the events of the night before, I could go to school and play with my friends, I could be a normal child doing normal childhood things, except of course mine was anything but. This suppression of the abuse served me well, but as I got older, I became very observant of my friends. I noticed what they wore and how they behaved. It was strong in me, the need to fit in and be like everyone else. That was never going to be entirely possible, but I did have a few successes with the friendships I made, and through playing netball, which at least allowed me to pretend I was normal, even though I never really felt it. What I did feel though, was more and more isolated and different from everyone around me, as time went by.

I always felt as if I was on my own, even when surrounded by family or friends. Even when there was noise and constant movement around, I felt removed from it. I now get that sense of isolation was due to the horrendous abuse I suffered, alongside being abandoned and neglected by both my parents at such a young age. Feeling different shadowed me throughout those years. I felt detached and removed—an outsider. When I did fit in, and I could do it convincingly, it felt forced and never rang true. I would dress the same as my friends, read the same magazines, eat the same junk food, but no matter how hard I tried to be just like them, I never felt I quite mastered it. I would be at their houses, study their families, the way their parents behaved towards them and wish I was them. I felt ashamed of my family, embarrassed about my home and alienated from everyone.

I didn't fit in my own family and wasn't welcome to, interestingly, I didn't fit in my friendships but was always welcome to. Part of the reason was that on the inside I felt so removed from their carefree worlds and families, so unutterably altered that I could never see a way to become a part of who they were. I was damaged and confused and couldn't understand why.

I have since come to learn that one of the key hallmarks of prolonged sexual abuse is 'feeling different'.

MEMORIES

I was thirty-two years old when the nightmares began.

I didn't understand what I was experiencing at the time as I had entirely blocked out my childhood. The first one woke me out of a deep sleep, terrified and shaking. My mind was awash with images of a skeleton at the door and an evil presence shrouded in a black cloak clutching a scythe in his hand. I was so sure it was real that I went to the front door and opened it, expecting to see it standing before me, ready to take me. The vision of death and destruction haunted me for the rest of the night and kept me from sleep. Over the next few weeks, I was to have this nightmare several more times, each one scarier than the last. About a month later, they began to escalate with a clear message: death was coming for me and there was no escape. It always involved bone-shattering terror, entrapment and no possibility of escape. I didn't understand what was happening to me and began to feel very alarmed. As I had two small children at the time, these surfacing nightmares were not welcome, so I tried hard to keep them at bay.

I would stay awake until late in the night trying to keep busy until exhaustion hit and my eyes would involuntarily close. I was fearful, tired and overwhelmed, yet I had no control over what was happening to me. I willed myself to stop having these fear-inducing dreams to no avail. I later understood my mind had decided I was ready to face the truth, whether I wanted to or not.

I now know we are always geared towards healing and wholeness, and as more and more revealed itself to me, I realised I had no choice but to embrace it until I was in possession of whatever these nightmares were trying to tell me. This was, without a doubt, a very frightening time in my adult life. More and more images emerged through the nightmares. Initially, I thought it was just odd, until faces and situations started appearing, then I realised something more powerful was at play. I went into therapy. I started to talk about what I was seeing, and it was during my fourth session that the words 'my father sexually abused me' tumbled out and hung there in the air. That seemed to unlock the door to thousands of memories which started to surface at a hundred miles an hour. It was a traumatising and unwanted experience and the beginning of what would turn out to be years of recall and recovery. I had many nights where I would wake sweating and shaking with terror, and days where I couldn't remember how I got through them. I felt lonely, unloved and terrified, much like I did during the first sixteen years of my life.

Alongside the memories were the flashbacks, the memories of past trauma. They took the form of snippets of pictures, sounds, smells, body sensations, feelings, or a numbing lack of them. I also had a sense of panic, of being trapped, a feeling of powerlessness with no memory stimulating them. These experiences also regularly appeared in my dreams. It was not uncommon for me to wake with the taste of semen in my mouth.

These horrendous flashbacks emerged seemingly from nowhere. I would be walking and suddenly see men behind me chasing me. I would look back, ready to run, yet no one was there. I would sometimes taste blood or have the image of being dragged along the ground by my hair. It got so bad that I even challenged some men who walked up my driveway, thinking they were coming to attack me. They weren't, they were just doing some surveying of the area.

My world became disjointed and unsafe. I began to viscerally experience the flashbacks as though they were happening in that moment. I didn't trust anyone nor share with many what I was going through. It was all I could do to survive this and care for my children. As a single mother with no real support, it was my goal to just get through each day.

I continued with therapy as more and more memories were coaxed out into the open, each one more unwelcome than the last. After sixteen years of trauma, there were thousands upon thousands of them. I know it surprised me that so much had happened which I had forgotten, until my therapist explained that repressing memories of trauma and abuse was the mind's way of protecting me from things that were too painful to deal with. A good analogy is of experiencing a bad car accident. People cannot usually recall what happened straight after the fact, it is too much for the mind to cope with, so the mind forms a protective barrier between the event and the recall to prevent the trauma from sinking in and causing further hurt. Its powerful and real and I am so grateful for it. I had endured sixteen years of prolonged, dangerous and traumatic events, and I am glad I didn't have conscious memory of it while I was a child. I don't think I would be here if I had.

Clearly, I was ready to face the truth, as the door opened and the memories surfaced. Over the next few years that became my daily life, dealing with the practicalities of raising small children and assimilating and processing the memories of my own childhood. I both wanted and didn't want to face my past. It was as if I was reliving the trauma, and life felt almost impossible. Adding to that was the dawning realisation that if I had been hoping for support and love from my family regarding my childhood, I was never going to receive it.

Several events occurred over those few years that remain implanted in my mind as the litany of lies that kept the abuse buried. The person I initially approached regarding the memories was my mother. Her first words accompanied by finger pointing were, 'You have no right to tell the others about this,' referring to my siblings. When asked why she said, 'They have a right to have a relationship with their father.' When I looked dubious, she earnestly began her manipulation, starting with, 'Are you sure you've got this right? The mind can play tricks on you.' I was shocked to realise she had no interest in supporting me, that it was all about keeping quiet and brushing the truth under the family carpet.

At the time, I didn't understand it; her lack of interest and concern was so palpable. Her main objective seemed to be shutting me down at all costs, the price of which I was to pay over the next twenty-five years. Now, I realise this is standard cover-up behaviour to ensure the truth is never exposed. The courage it took me to tell her was beyond significant. Regardless, she discounted it immediately. How could she be so callous and disregard how bad I felt? My trauma from the abuse heightened and I began to regress. I felt like my teenage self all over again. I was frightened, anxious and sad, which caused my mother to respond not with love and kindness, but with anger and frustration. She had no interest in what I was going through other than to manipulate me to stop the truth spreading. Because I had been made out to be wrong again so quickly, she had not bothered to see what it cost me to speak up, let alone any possible gain in me doing so. It really would have surprised her to learn that I didn't want anything from her, apart from love and support.

Instead, I received nothing but judgement and dismissal. I was both confused and devastated by her response. She seemed more concerned at how it may impact her image out in the community rather than the impact it had on me. Naively, I held onto the hope she would believe me and support me.

Over time, I realised if she hadn't been there for me as a child, she wouldn't be there for me as an adult. Towards the end of that initial conversation, she insisted on knowing if I would be telling my siblings, hoping I wouldn't. I said I would be with my rationale being: it happened to them as well and they had a right to know the truth. She was furious. Her whole face changed dramatically, but I was determined they should at least hear my story and hopefully I would get to hear theirs. This did not turn out as expected either, which shouldn't have come as a surprise but did.

Because of their long-held attitudes of disappointment and disregard for me, it had been hard to maintain meaningful relationships with my siblings. I had always felt a measure of suspicion and caution from them. Although we tried, we didn't really connect. Over the years, we saw each other at family events, but no closeness was formed between us. I found it difficult to relate to any of them, as they were so different from me and seemed to only tolerate me. Without exception, they had all turned to fundamentalist Christianity which further cemented their worldview. I felt judged and wrong around them and part of me could not accept that level of rejection anymore. The differences between us grew and their view of me as 'the different one' became entrenched. Although I knew my sisters loved me underneath it all, it was always overlaid with thinly veiled disappointment and judgement.

My siblings had all married within a year of each other and were seemingly as much in love with the church as with their spouses. This was not, nor could it have ever been, my path, as I always felt like I didn't need to be told how to think—I could do that for myself. I would have loved to have been closer to them, but I just did not feel welcome unless I chose to give up my non-religious outlook and embrace their unquestioning faith.

I don't blame my siblings for their choices, but what I do hold them accountable for is their betrayal when I approached them about the abuse I suffered. I had optimistically assumed they would be shocked and supportive and stand by me once they heard the truth. What I had failed to factor in was they would never be able to do that if my mother didn't. They didn't have the courage to go against her. She was a master manipulator, and they were just the pawns in her game. Looking back, they never stood a chance in standing up for, let alone supporting, me. Once my mother was aware that I had approached my siblings, she started playing her game and pulled all of her moves to ensure they retracted any positive or truthful statement they had made in support of me. This fresh targeted rejection cut me deeply.

Initially, my brother, Shane, said he wanted to believe me, but he couldn't bear to think his father, let alone himself, had done anything like that. He became very quiet and withdrawn and bluntly told me not to discuss it with him again. That was his stance, one he held onto so strongly that our relationship became irreparably broken. I was devastated by this, as he was the only other sibling that had lived with me for those eighteen months, so he would surely have more memories of our childhood events than the others. I wasn't blaming him or angry with him, rather I was his broken younger sister who needed his support and love. However, he was much more like my mother than either of us realised, and the truth could never be revealed because it would mean he would have to face into what he and his friends had done to me. That was never going to happen, despite it contradicting the foundational principles of his newfound Biblical beliefs. 'Then you will know the truth, and the truth will set you free'—John 8:32. It was easier for Shane to have me scapegoated than for him to face up to his torture and rape of me over so many years.

My sister, Debbie, initially said she believed me, but she couldn't really remember anything from her childhood. She told me that she had no doubt I was telling the truth and was saddened by what I said—that was until my mother influenced her and she denied ever saying it. I told her I hoped the truth would be revealed to her one day so she could deal with her own traumatic memories and be healed of it all. To have her turn her back on me was a new level of rejection as I had always found her to be kinder than the others. Her believing me, then back-tracking was a lot to grapple with at a difficult time in my life. However, we all have choices, and it was easier to for her to go with the status quo than to stand up for what was right.

It was my eldest sister, Chris, who said to me, 'I knew something terrible was happening to you in that house when you were left there with him. I just knew it.' She was the most supportive and helpful of all until I noticed she didn't want to discuss it or meet with me anymore. I found out my mother had spoken to her. Chris completely retracted her statement and denied she had ever said anything like that. She surprised me the most with this, as when she was younger, she had proven herself strong enough to stand up to our mother. But once again, in a scenario where I was right, I was made out to be wrong. I couldn't stomach the pity Chris showed to me after that.

It wasn't enough that my mother had got to them and they had recanted their statements. She had to take it to another level. She undertook research, strategised, amassed an army of troops around her and came up with the following: 'I believe you believe this happened to you, but this is simply false memory syndrome.' She went on to tell me that it was not my fault, but to continue on this self-destructive path would only cause pain for everyone around me. I should have realised she would do whatever it took to stop me. It had shocked her to realise the others may actually want to believe me and support me. Over the ensuing months, they all began to label me as deluded and easily manipulated. The psychologist I had seen was labelled 'the manipulator', the one who had planted these 'lies' in my head. God, of course, was also thrown in there and I just couldn't compete with that.

They told me they wanted to pray over me and have the delusion removed from my heart. My siblings seemed genuinely worried about me, having totally swallowed my mother's scheming and scapegoating so as to think I was seriously mentally ill. I got promoted from 'the black sheep' to 'the pitied one', which became my new identity that they gladly touted and feverishly prayed over. I was 'the unfortunate one', 'the one who didn't have God', 'the one who needed their forgiveness'.

My mother appeared delighted by how well her plan had worked. The spotlight was off her and any responsibility she should have carried was thrown straight back at me.

To say I was upset and overwhelmed doesn't begin to cover it, as not only had my family turned their backs on me, but they had now made me out to be an unstable object of pity, one step short of needing a miracle from God. I felt that if it was a viable option, my mother would have manipulated the Catholic Church to somehow make it happen. That's how determined she was the truth could never be exposed. It was obvious she was never going to allow any scandal to erupt with her name attached. Once again, I became the scapegoat, and once again, I was turned bad. The cycle was complete, all was as it should be. I was wrong and lying, they were right and honourable. Looking back, my siblings never stood a chance. I couldn't force them to stand by me, when they were clearly under orders not to. Initially, I think my sisters did try, but my mother was much too powerful a force for them to battle.

My siblings stayed in touch with me until it became clear that I would not retract my stance on the abuse, then they withdrew more and more. At one stage, Debbie approached me, directed to by my mother, and asked me if I enjoyed being 'the black sheep' of the family. She said if I could just repent my sins, God would welcome me with open arms. What sins? What did I have to repent? What had I done that was so wrong I needed forgiveness? My mistake was daring to tell the truth and asking for support. In their eyes I became wrong and selfish, which closely resembled how they had seen me throughout most of my childhood. I shouldn't really have been surprised, but I was.

What they failed to see back then was that I had nothing to gain by speaking out and telling the truth. There was no reward in it for me, no recognition I sought. Rather, I longed for solidarity and compassion from the only people who could possibly understand what those years were truly like: my siblings.

They had always been manipulated and controlled by my mother and, for much of my life, I had been too. It was a normal part of having her love, letting her decide what was real or not, deciding what was true or not. It was also easier and less painful as going against her was too damaging and annihilating for me. She would make me pay by removing her love, as she had proven many times over my childhood and adolescence. On this matter, I couldn't let that happen and of that I am proud. It would have been so much easier if I could have just given in, pretended I had it wrong or lied to keep the peace, it should have been simple for me to do as I had spent my whole life keeping her secrets and pretending, but time was up. Simply put I couldn't allow this to continue anymore. I had sacrificed my whole life up until that point by living a lie, supressing the truth and the feelings it brought up. The die had been cast and I had to just watch it roll and see the consequences it had on my world and my children's.

Awareness grew in me, strongly indicating that I would need greater courage than what I already possessed, alongside solid support to withstand the reactions and behaviour of the family. I was fortunate to have wonderful friends in my life, but I needed some help beyond that, so I turned to spirituality once again, which led me to the work of authors Louise Hay and Wayne Dwyer. They became my teachers and guides and it was through them I reconnected with the deeper part of myself and drew in a wonderful lawyer, doctor and psychologist, all of whom helped me to unpack what was happening and supported me in piecing together the story of my life.

HOME

In order to contextualise the abuse within our home, it is important to revisit my parents' history up until their separation, including how our family had functioned during those sixteen formative years.

My parents were both born and raised in Auckland, New Zealand, both with large families. My mother's family originated from Scotland, my father's from Ireland. Both families were diehard Catholic, and that is how my parents met, through the Catholic Church.

Back in the 1950s, dates were chaperoned. My parents met at a youth dance held in a local church hall. When they dated afterwards, they were accompanied by my maternal grandmother as chaperone. She would sit in the back seat of the car while my mother and father sat in the front, driving around the waterfront in Auckland. This was standard protocol for the times, and I don't believe they even had an hour alone together before they became engaged. From my father's family's perspective, perhaps it was time to settle down, find the right girl and start a family. I think in the beginning they did love each other, and that there was something more than duty and social pressure that bound them together. I hope so anyway.

When they married in 1953, my mother was twenty and my father was twenty-three. I'm sure it was a happy day and celebration for both of them. I'm equally sure they had high hopes of a long and happy union full of many wonderful memories to make and share. They did what was expected at the time: they met, married and had a large family all quite quickly.

Our family didn't socialise that much, though occasionally friends would arrive over for drinks and a singsong around the piano. It was unusual for two reasons: the house got cleaned, and my parents became completely different people. They were friendly, smiling and warm to all who entered their home. Nothing was too much trouble. The socialising was usually with people from the church, or friends from the tennis club. I don't know if they ever let anyone get particularly close, but they seemed to smile and enjoy the company. Usually, our family would go to their houses for lunch or dinner and we would play with their children while the adults sat around drinking and laughing. Although my father was a big drinker—really, he was an alcoholic —my mother rarely drank, claiming she was allergic and that it made her sick. I think what she got out of these get-togethers was the enjoyment of seeing her friends and talking about herself. I know she looked forward to those outings so she could engage with people who were interested in her. I, on the other hand, looked forward to those outings because the houses were usually warm, there were toys to play with and there was nice food to eat.

Other social activities tended to be with extended family. We used to go to Nana B's a lot to see my father's family and occasionally to visit my mothers'. The difference between the two family dynamics was significant. At Nana B's, it was more relaxed and we were welcomed, whereas at my maternal grandparents' home the atmosphere was austere and strict, with no real warmth shown to any of us children.

There were many times throughout my childhood years when it was all too much. In the early days, it was sad and confusing, and I felt like I was always in trouble for something. I wondered why I was so hated and used to dream that somehow I had it wrong and they did love me. Then I would wake up and reality would hit, usually in the form of a beating or being sent to my room for most of the day. When I wasn't in trouble, the usual routine was for us girls to 'entertain ourselves' in the form of 'go outside and play'. I would have been about four at the time, and I knew we would not be allowed back inside the house before dinnertime which was around 6 pm. I remember being so tired that Christine would have to carry me inside because I just needed to go to bed. I was only little after all. The difference between how us girls and Shane were treated was like comparing black to white. The contrast was stark. He never had to lift a finger, as we girls were expected to do everything for him. I don't know how Christine got to do her homework at night, as she would have been exhausted after caring for us all afternoon and then trying to help cook dinner and feed us.

Sometimes, for no apparent reason, we would be locked outside for hours at a time without access to a toilet or food. We were used to being hungry, but not having a bathroom posed a problem. I think my father would use this as punishment for some perceived misdemeanour, but for my mother I think it was just a relief as it meant she didn't have to see us. The problem was that we were children and could only rely on our mother's care and protection. I was often confused and anxious around what we had done to deserve being locked out again. If I hadn't had my sisters and the gregarious and curious personality I did, I don't think I would have survived my childhood.

The bizarre and extreme abuse occurred daily and everyone was a target. The impact on each of us varied in accordance with our personalities. We tended to manage by adapting as best as we could to the situation. Christine would take charge and shepherd us girls into a space away from The Monster to protect us from further harm. This only worked for so long and though she tried her best, even she couldn't keep us safe forever. I noticed that as she got older, she would get angry quite quickly. The shift in her from soft-natured and sweet, to angry and frustrated happened when she was about eleven.

Christine's key objective had always been to protect us and if we were too noisy, she would try to distract us, so we learned to be very quiet and hypervigilant. She would try to pretend that it was all okay in order to reassure us, but the impact on her was becoming harder to bear. She would become increasingly angry and resentful towards our mother because she was the safest person to whom she could vent her feelings. Although this would have had an impact, over time nothing really changed and she became more lost to herself. The light within my eldest sister started to dim, until it eventually flickered and died out.

Debbie's way of coping was to withdraw from the outside world. She became adept at that, not out of choice, but out of fear. She was very scared around my father and if she heard him either driving down the driveway or walking towards her, she would become even quieter and retreat into herself, almost to the point where she couldn't move or hide. I knew she would often freeze and therefore be an easy target, but I didn't know how to help her. She tended to be in a dissociative state and didn't seem quite there, eventually I began to realise her freeze mentality would override her awareness of whether he was home or not. If he was there, I would try to distract her by playing little finger shadow games. Making pictures with my hands against the light reflected on the wall would make her smile, and I would do anything to make her smile. I didn't realise it back then, but I was really trying to keep her out of harm's way.

Shane was another story entirely. Since he was a boy, he had no fear of retribution or punishment from my father. He could loudly and forcefully strut about the house, do whatever he wanted to us and never suffer any consequences. Although his home life was different to ours, he couldn't escape the abuse unscathed. Whether or not he was the 'prince' in our home, he observed and took part in many abhorrent, degrading sexual attacks on my sisters and me. Although, at times, he appeared to be a reluctant participant, he was made to observe and partake in these acts. As he got older and matured, the depravity and violence seemed to become more and more enjoyable for him. In the end, he was the 'mini-me' of my father and I don't underestimate the psychological impact this would have had on him. I always keep in mind that for him it began when he was a small child, with no choice. However, as a young adult, he always had a choice.

For me, as the youngest, I started to doubt myself and would copy what Debbie or Christine did. I would usually hide behind them and follow them around. My personality was such that I was a positive, noisy little girl and so this 'shutting down' was out of character for me. I was traumatised and fearful and there was no safe place for me. I tended to do what they did and kept as quiet and small as possible. Eventually though my protective and nurturing side took over and I would work hard at trying to keep them out of harm's way, or as much as I could anyway.

I know what really helped me was being able to notice the beauty in things especially the light in the sky. It felt like it was seeking me out, as it was always there just waiting for me to come and play with it. I would see shapes in the clouds and feel happy. I would notice a rainbow through the window, and when the abuse was over, I would run and run to find the pot of gold I knew was waiting for me at the end. My biggest saviours were my Angels, typically appearing as lights in the sky. They always gave me something I never had outside of my imagination: hope, and in my world, hope was everything.

Alongside the daily trauma, I also suffered vicarious traumatisation which means being traumatised by watching others being hurt or abused. This happened on a regular basis and there was nothing scarier than watching my father hurt my mother. The violence and abuse towards her were there for long as I could remember. My father would call her names, taunt and diminish her. She would stand her ground, but this would often escalate into nasty, violent arguments during which he pushed her around. Us children would become very quiet during those times and try to slink away unnoticed, but this would just enrage my father further, as he wanted all of us to suffer his psychopathic fury. He loved an audience, holding us to ransom and seeing the terror on our faces.

My mother never discussed what happened during those years. She may have blocked it out because it was just too much for her to remember or revisit. She would often say to my father, 'Not in front of the children,' but this would just stoke his fire. He would yell at her about how useless she was, call her fat, get my brother to join in the nastiness and thoroughly enjoy the impact he was having on all of us. If one of us girls tried to distract him or save Mum in some way we would be dragged by our hair across the room, pulled across the kitchen by our ear or flung against a wall. The violence and aggression became normal and much worse as I became older. There was one night in particular where he had a knife against her throat, only stopping because the phone rang. I believe whoever phoned that night saved her from serious injury or worse.

It is an understatement to say our home was unhappy. It was plain miserable, particularly when the marriage between my parents broke down hideously. Extreme aggression and dysfunctional behaviour were normalised. Their union was not a match made in heaven, but in hell, forged out of blame and bitterness, with no bond of love between them. Our home was a toxic and uncaring environment, and either one of them was typically absent for long periods of time to avoid not just each other, but us.

NARCISSIST

Among other things, a narcissist is someone with an inflated sense of their own importance, harbouring a deep need for constant, excessive attention and admiration and a lack of empathy for others. I'm sure my mother was one.

Throughout my entire life, her self-projected image was everything to her and it became her addiction. The web of deceit and lies she spun over the years became more and more entrenched in her mind until she saw them as facts. Her view was the truth. The real truth didn't matter. Her history does not excuse choices she made as an adult, as she knew what she was doing every single day of her adult life, and those actions remain her legacy.

I had been told that she was sent away from her family to live with her maternal grandmother when she was three years old. Apparently, my grandmother was struggling with ill health, had a younger toddler to care for and was heavily pregnant with her third child. She was not coping, often had chronic asthma and felt the demands of her eldest were too much, so my mother was sent to live with her grandmother. My grandfather was not mentioned in this decision making so I have no idea whether he agreed with it or not. Regardless of who said what, that was my mother's start in life.

From what my mother told me, the home she was sent to was devoid of affection or kindness. She was to be 'seen and not heard'. There was no room for her to be a playful, inquisitive three-year-old, and I imagine she quickly learned to adapt to her new surroundings. She was living with my great-grandmother, great-grandfather and great aunt, Edna. They were described as strict Catholics with no capacity for childlike abandon and imagination. She apparently was only shown interest or care when she was sick. So sick she would become. Once I learned how many childhood illnesses and ailments had plagued her throughout her younger life, I wondered if this was the beginning of the hypochondriac tendencies she embraced fully when she became a mother.

To my knowledge, she was allowed to visit her family home and see her sisters occasionally, and although she yearned to live there with them, she was not allowed to move back home until she was twelve years old.

I know the loneliness and isolation would have been challenging for my mother, let alone the confusion. She told me once that she adapted by being quiet and learning how to entertain herself. She also learned who to approach for attention and praise. This was rarely given, so she tried to earn it as best she could. Being sent away at such a young age and raised by strict and judgemental grandparent's must have been very tough. To have lived with them for nine years would have meant she became part of her surroundings and felt this was her real home.

When I think of her at age twelve, finally being able to reintegrate into the family home without the natural authority the eldest child possesses, I realise how difficult that must have been. I never did find out why that was that was deemed the right age, though. While I felt incredibly sad that my mother experienced such deliberate rejection herself from such a young age, it highlights how intergenerational neglect and abandonment repeat themselves. Despite having undergone all of that, she chose to replicate that behaviour when she became a mother herself. Although what she went through must have been scary and lonely, it doesn't excuse her complicit and enabling pattern of behaviour which rendered me a helpless child victim to a dangerous paedophile. But what it does do, is help contextualise my mother's complete lack of love, kindness, or empathy towards me.

After all, she had not experienced it herself, so how could she possibly show it to me? What I do know is we parent the way we were unless we choose not to. History really does repeat itself, as I was also twelve years old when I returned to live with my mother.

The narrative my mother recounted regarding being turfed out of the family home at such a tender age and stage in life has always struck me as odd. She idealised her mother, describing her as a wonderful, compassionate and wise woman while completely ignoring or minimising her decision to send her away.

Never once did I hear her acknowledge any sense of rejection or sadness about that time. The fact that my mother could only see her mother as kind, wise and loving reveals the level of narcissistic wounding she experienced. She could only ever see her parents as God-like and almost saintly in their words and deeds. I didn't see that in them and wondered why. My experience of them, especially of my grandmother, was one of rejection and disdain. She didn't like me, didn't want me in her house and suffered my presence much as you would an unwanted pet.

My mother grew up in Onehunga and later moved to Cornwall Park. She was the eldest of four girls and went to Catholic schools throughout her childhood and adolescence. Although she was highly intelligent and competent, she never completed her final exams and, in fact, left without finishing sixth form. I was well into my forties before that information came to light. As it was such a well-guarded secret, I wonder what really happened to her that year.

It was only a few years later when my mother chose to marry my father. Marrying young was the norm then, as was marrying a likeminded peer from limited circles at church, sporting or social clubs. What should have been a wonderful and exciting journey of two becoming one and building a shared life together instead became a nightmare for my parents, and subsequently for us.

To be the youngest child born into that dysfunction was frightening. I tended to be ignored or chastised with nothing in between. I was lucky as a baby that I learned to cry loudly because it meant I would at times receive some measure of attention from my mother. She often seemed angry that I needed feeding or changing, except for when she was putting on a motherly front for other people. I think if she could have sent me away somewhere, she would have, but, to save face, she couldn't. Narcissists have an image to maintain, so I stayed put. I was lucky to have had Christine who always had to look after me and would come running if I started crying. Even though she was only a child herself, I felt her genuine love and concern.

My mother never once put me first unless I was really ill. It was more common to find the house empty and the cupboards bare when I got home from school than to have her at home waiting for me. She would go and stay at her mother's house in Remuera to 'recover' from some perceived or real illness. I think the thought of caring for and loving four children was too much for her, especially the needy youngest one. Plus, she didn't seem to like me very much. She was expected to cope, but she didn't know how, so she chose 'plan B' and gave up on me essentially from the time I was born.

Fortunately, a lady from the parish helped to care for our family, and I think she may have been the only person who truly liked me. My mother was excellent socially and faked her love for me convincingly. To most outsiders, I was just naughty and demanding and should have been grateful to have had such a lovely mum. Outwardly, she was a beautiful woman with a great personality and charming social skills and that was all people saw, which is exactly how she wanted it. Inwardly, she resented me for existing and I felt that daily.

Narcissism is a complex and debilitating disorder, not necessarily for the narcissist themselves, but for their family and friends. As a child of a narcissist, my needs were at best secondary to my mother's, but more often just ignored. I had to find my own way and learn how to be in the world. This is in part why I became 'the carer'. It meant me looking out for her, not the other way around. The psychological term for this is 'the parentified child' and it certainly seemed to fit what I learned to do. I would always be offering to help her, to get her something, to run to the dairy for her. Whatever she required, I learned quickly to be the one to do it. That way I might get some attention, otherwise I got nothing. When she reached out to tell me I was a 'good girl', it was worth the resentment and frustration I received from her at all other times. If I could just keep giving and keeping her happy, she might even like me a little bit, or so I hoped.

My mother's narcissist tendencies knew no bounds. She considered herself to be more attractive and intelligent than others and usually spent a lot of time and effort curating both her appearance and social interactions. People would comment on her personality and immaculate dress sense, whilst ignoring that her four children had seriously outgrown all their clothes, were wearing hand me downs and were dirty and smelly. However, as good Catholic families did, we went to church on Sundays and put on a holy act. No one was any the wiser, or if they were, no one intervened.

Because of her chaotic and miserable marriage coupled with extreme self-absorption, my mother was uninterested in dealing with the prolonged and unending sexual abuse I suffered at the hands of my father. In retrospect, it seemed she was just relieved The Monster wanted to put me to bed or follow me to the bedroom. This evolved further into taking me out for hours on end, or to sleepovers at his mother's house. She loved the fact that if I wasn't there, she didn't have to give me any attention; she could focus on herself instead. This suited her far more than having to keep an eye out on the youngest child who she considered naughty and needy. Over time, as the abuse worsened, I became more withdrawn. My mother, however, became more and more caught up in the glowing reviews she received from others about herself and her work. Over the course of her career, she experienced great success in New Zealand, becoming something of a pioneering self-help guru in the 1980s. She was eminently successful and considered herself to be something of a local legend. She was very influential in helping a lot of people fulfil their potential and her books sold well.

She was chosen as a keynote speaker at events, went on book signing tours and was a mentor to several businesses. Unfortunately, she wasn't able to translate that same dedication and commitment in her professional life to her parenting. Although we were older when she achieved her fame, she was working hard towards this when we were younger. As small children, we were not cared for and, in fact, neglect and abandonment were the more common themes permeating our household.

As well as being a complex narcissist, she was also a class-A chronic enabler. She did this in many ways and through key relationships, the most damaging being my father and his abuse of me. By being so detached and disinterested, she could only see herself and her needs and these became of paramount importance. All of her energy was channelled into encouraging situations where her self-interest could be met. She made it very obvious that she had no concern for me, and was unconsciously enabling him to abuse and use me whenever and however he wanted.

A good example of this was when my father would suggest taking me away and out of her sight, she would always be grateful and relieved about that. For her this meant she could both forget about and have a break from me. What was strange about this was that I was never front of mind for her anyway. She never noticed I was shaking or crying or wanting to hide whenever my father came home or came near me. She never saw that I would cling to her with trembling hands, on shaky legs, begging her not to let him put me to bed. She never noticed the desperation or vulnerability in me, never really cared enough to look. The hardest thing to accept was that she never actually had any empathy or real compassion towards me at all. Ever.

Until I was an adult, but by then it was far too late.

I was always considered to be in the way and a nuisance to her and remained so until I didn't need her anymore, around the age of seventeen. The only time she ever took notice of me was when there was something in it for her. If I could look after her in some way, I would be seen as 'the good child' or 'the helpful one'. So, as children do, I adapted and made sure to perfect this image throughout my childhood years. If I could do something for her and help look after her in some way, I would do it.

What I struggled with, and was truly hard to accept, was the severe impact of her neglect and abandonment of me from such a young age. Since I had such limited awareness of what was really going on, I had always held the illusion that one day, she would magically look after me and love me.

That day never arrived.

As a child growing up around such extreme narcissism, I found it hard to find things to look forward to, but as I knew Mum loved Christmas, that was something I looked forward to as well. One of the differences between adults and children is magical thinking, believing in things like the tooth fairy and Santa. Christmas was a big deal and one of the few times I would hopefully get a present. At school we would spend weeks making Christmas cards and presents for our families and loved ones, believing that if we were good, we would get some presents too.

The inevitable truth was that in our household there was no celebration, no festive food or special toys. That was only if we went to visit extended family, otherwise it was just another day in misery-land. It didn't seem to count that we were long standing members of the Catholic Church who viewed Christmas as a time for love, family and celebration. The atmosphere in our household could not have been less joy filled. The most wonderful time of year was a difficult time, made even more so by neighbours and friends showing off their new shiny toys in the street. I can recall a couple of times over my entire childhood when we had presents and new toys to play with. For the most part though, we were left empty-handed with no Santa sacks to open. It was just a horrible day with us being instructed to lie to people should they ask what we got for Xmas. I remember one year, I would have been about seven, talking to the neighbours. As they asked what gifts I received, I plastered a smile on my face, frantically trying to describe my new toys which, in reality, were non-existent.

My mother told me in later years that she had always wanted to buy us presents but The Monster refused to allow it. Whatever the actual truth was, all I know is that I felt shame and guilt at having to pretend to others that I was given presents. I would have loved the latest doll to play with, but that was never ever going to happen. To be frank, I probably would have been thrilled with just having nice food to eat. I do believe my mother wanted to celebrate Christmas, but I am unsure of her real motive. If it had suited her, it would have been quite the occasion. As it was, later in the day she would escape to her parents' home to be spoilt and loved, while we were left behind with him. I'm sure that as she opened her presents under the Christmas tree with her family, she didn't give us a second thought. I'm equally sure that while she was tucking into roast turkey with all the trimmings, she wasn't mourning her children's empty tummies.

Because my mother was so disinterested in caring for me, I felt hungry most of the time and learned to do anything to get food. One of the more successful ways I managed this was waiting until she was in the bedroom with the door closed before raiding her purse in the kitchen to race down to the dairy and buy treats. I knew that once she was in that room with the door shut, she would be in there for hours. The rule was she was *never* to be disturbed upon threat of death! I would have been as young as three when she first laid down this law.

Believe it or not, those were some of the few times I felt happy. I was happy because I could eat chocolate and happy because I had food. Because my mother was so shut off to me and I was so hungry, I felt justified in doing this. I guess knowing the bedroom door was usually closed meant that she wouldn't come out anytime soon. So, I was safe to get away with it and so I kept doing it. I would make sure to check on her bedroom door, then run like the wind to the dairy to buy sinful, gorgeous treats. I felt magical amidst the thievery and gluttony, truly alive in those moments. It was one way to get my tummy filled and feel some sort of happiness. It wasn't going to come from my mother as she had made abundantly clear: she was not available. At all. Ever. Do not disturb.

Underneath it all, the truth was that I missed my mother so much. Even when she was actually at home, she wasn't home to me, and if she was away, I never knew when or if she was coming back. As a young one, I didn't know if she had died or was away or what had happened to her. I just never saw her much and she clearly didn't want to see me. I'm pretty sure my grandmother's house was her haven. It felt like she lived there and would visit us from time to time. My mother had such prolonged absences from our lives that I used to wonder if she really did exist. I would sit on the driveway hoping she would magically appear and show me she loved me. I was just little and didn't understand what was happening, but I knew I wanted my mummy. I used to pray that God would bring her home and that she would be nice to me. I don't know whether God was busy in those days, but neither of those things happened. The impact on me was to turn myself bad, as if my own mother couldn't stand to be near me, I must be a wickedly bad child.

NB: There is no such thing as a wicked or bad child. Rather, it is the adults around them who treat them as if they are, until the child believes it is true and acts accordingly. Under my mother's influence, it became easier for me to see myself as wicked and bad rather than the beautiful and innocent child I was.

PSYCHOPATH

I have very limited knowledge of my father's background, simply because it wasn't discussed. When we visited my paternal grandparents' house, the focus was never on their history, but on safe topics like work and family. When my mother wasn't with us, the conversation turned to how more money could be made from me being trafficked to others.

From an early age, I knew my mother did not like my father's family, particularly the way his mother treated her. Nana B was never all that interested in my mother. She would make sure the conversation revolved around my father and expected my mother to sit back and applaud his every word. In the end, my mother would avoid going to Nana B's home at all costs, but when she had no choice, she would reluctantly accompany us. I knew she didn't like going there because of how she would talk about it later, both in front of my father and behind his back. She would act the dutiful daughter-in-law in front of my grandmother but was never happy to be around her. I sensed the feeling was mutual as Nana B used to 'cluck' a lot and pull a disapproving face whenever she saw her.

My grandfather didn't feature much and remains quite a mystery as he died when I was about three. My mother told me he was friendly and warm and treated her kindly. I personally have no memory of him, apart from thinking he seemed nicer than my grandmother.

Apparently, my father, the psychopath, was remarkably talented and capable of almost anything. He was lauded as being 'special' and 'chosen'. I used to wonder what that meant, thinking he must have achieved great things. After much research and study of his life, the sole reason for his 'superior' status appeared to be that he was the only boy in his Irish Catholic family!

My father was raised in Kingsland, Auckland, on a shabby suburban street in a house that looked much the same as all the others. He was educated at local private Catholic schools, and did not attend university, but rather he studied the art of plumbing which became his career. Privileged and treated very differently from his sisters, he ended up a psychopath.

Growing up, his sisters were made to wait on him hand and foot, even tying his shoelaces and handfeeding him. I was told they were repeatedly admonished for not doing enough for him. They were not allowed to eat before he had finished eating, and in fact, the best parts of any meal were always given to him to the point where he would be specially served the more expensive cuts of meat. My aunties were reportedly shut down, berated, kicked and sometimes beaten by him for some perceived wrongdoing. It could have been anything or nothing—there never needed to be an excuse, but some of those given were that they hadn't cleaned his room, hadn't offered to prepare his food or they hadn't moved out of 'his chair'. All were unacceptable and therefore punishable. For my father growing up, society reinforced his male superiority.

The Catholic Church in part contributed to this through their doctrine that the man was the head of the house. By 1960, when I was born, not only had he been primed to victimise and abuse his own siblings, but us as well. Combine that with the view against contraception during the

50s and 60s and it was a powder keg waiting to explode. Large families were the norm in Catholic circles. Having four children under six would be a feat most young couples would struggle with, and my parents were no exception. The pressure and the exhaustion would have been enough to cause a ripple of disharmony in their marriage, which over time eventuated into huge rivers of dislike, blame and resentment.

The Monster, being unable to even tie his own shoelaces, could not possibly be expected to help his wife or assist with any 'women's work'. His view was siloed and patriarchal. He would go to work and do the outside jobs. She was expected to raise the family and be a slave to the house and to him. He could not see beyond that. As he had been raised to believe he was 'special' and 'chosen,' finding himself in an unhappy marriage with an unhappy woman and four young children would not have aligned with his self-image or befit his lofty status.

Naturally, we, his children, bore the brunt of his disappointment and rage as he turned our home into an environment of neglect, abandonment, and relentless beatings, abuse and suffering. Us children were left alone, unattended, unloved and unwanted for so long, by both of our parents, I'm not surprised we became dysfunctional ourselves. What choice did we have? It became the norm for us to cook, clean, run the household and do the outside work. As I was the youngest, I had no idea what I was doing and didn't do it all that well. I usually got it wrong and was violently punished for it.

As my parents' marriage deteriorated ever more rapidly, and the love they might have once had for one another morphed into resentment and eventually hate, it became normal to be left with our father. He seemed to forget or not acknowledge that he had four children, as he, too, would often leave, to party and drink with his friends, or worse still—bring them home. It appeared that once my mother was absent, it was open season with his paedophile friends. This was generally kept to weekends and holidays and never while she was there.

When I look back at his behaviour, his psychopathic tendencies were becoming more entrenched. The initial abuse was never going to be enough to satisfy him, so over time, the attacks became more sadistic. I came to learn that the cruel and deliberate methods of abuse he used would often feel more frightening than when he started involving other people.

As months went by and the depravity grew, I would do whatever he wanted. His physical size and fury were frightening enough, but the real damage was repeatedly being threatened with murder. As a child, naturally I believed every word he said.

He made sure I never knew at what point I would be ripped out of my bed, thrown into the van and driven to some destination unknown so he could sell me to his contacts through the club and other sex trafficking networks. I was often terrified and traumatised, and just wanted my mum.

Over time, The Monster's drug and alcohol abuse escalated. At home, he was always drunk or well on his way, and his drug-taking increased exponentially over the months. In those days, the '6 pm swill' was alive and well, so by the time he came home at night, he was already primed to be abusive and violent. His fury and resentment towards us girls and my mother escalated with many beatings. It was not uncommon for one of us to be punched or kicked, or even thrown off the deck if the mood took him. Anything could inflame him—with no warnings or apparent triggers, he would erupt. Sometimes he would encourage my brother to join in, replicating shades of his own history, so Shane would participate, often kicking and beating us as well. Although my mother may have tried to intervene occasionally, it wasn't often. Her interest was self-focused rather than child-focused. The weekends became a whole other story when my father enthusiastically became very drunk or returned home from a night out with his friends.

The Monster seemed to highly value others' opinions of him, whether workmates or drinking buddies. What better way to impress them than to get the latest 1968 blue chrome Pontiac on the market, imported all the way from America. As a family, we still couldn't afford to eat properly or have warm clothes, let alone shoes that fit and yet, surprisingly, we seemed to be able to afford a Pontiac and a brand new one at that. As a child, I wondered how that was even possible. I don't know how he rationalised it to people, as my mother constantly accepted handouts, but somehow he did. It now seems bizarre that no one questioned how he could afford a car like that.

The answer was through selling his own children for sex. I can't remember my mother's reaction to this car turning up, but I do know she was not happy and this was to become yet another bone of contention between them. His friends, however, loved it. It was yet another way for him to get some recognition as 'the man' and he made sure it was on show for all to see whenever they came around. Friends from work, the local tennis club, the Catholic Church and the underworld connections he formed would turn up to look at the car and congratulate him on it.

This would usually lead to him going out and coming home drunk many hours later. He was always wanting to socialise, as his personality was gregarious and therefore 'Mr Charm and Personality' when he needed to be. 'Mr B,' people would say to him, 'you're such a hoot!' Apart from family, no one ever really saw who he was unless he chose to reveal himself to them. To the day he died, I don't believe that would have been more than a handful of people.

During the week, my father was a relatively hard-working plumber. Although he had supreme authority over us, his behaviour and attitude didn't seem to command respect from others. I wonder if he had believed what he had been told growing up and was surprised people didn't treat him the way his family had? Maybe his adult life was a disappointment to him? I do wonder at the stories he would have had to tell himself to reconcile his childhood conditioning with the reality of his adult life. To gain his plumbing qualification, he trained for the required number of years, completed an apprenticeship and eventually started and operated his own business with reasonable success.

He had all the power and was the king of his domain. Aside from that, he was a very intelligent and clever man. I don't doubt that he was as talented and witty as my grandmother described him, as I'm certain he could have been anything he wanted. I'm also certain he could have chosen to follow a better path. I don't know what aspirations he had for his life, but whatever they were, he actively chose the life he led. Throughout my entire childhood, my father and I *never once* had a normal father-daughter conversation about life, goals, career, money, family, or love. No guidance, no protection, no fatherly pride or interest shown. The only time he ever gave me attention was to exploit, train, or condition me to become the best child prostitute I could be. One he could be proud of.

I don't believe he ever saw me for me.

As he was conditioned throughout his early life to become a monster, The Monster he became. Did he really have a choice when his own upbringing prophesied evil and all he did was fulfil it?

His reason for existing seemed to be to inflict harm on his children. Our misery and fear were recognition that he was good at what he did. He placed no value on himself and those he fathered. It leads me to wonder how much untapped and unrecognised potential there was in him.

SILENCE

Once I realised that child sexual abuse thrives in secrecy, I finally understood why my family had been so intent on shutting me down. They would do anything to cover this up and through their dogged perseverance they unwittingly helped confirm that the reason systemic and prolonged abuse continues to exist is due to the power of silence. Right from the first conversation in which I disclosed the abuse, my family's reaction defied belief. Over the next twenty-five years, their commitment to silence at all costs only became more entrenched.

I knew that my exposing our family history would not be welcomed by any of my family members, not least of all my mother, but what I hadn't accounted for was that I would be turned on and blamed without so much as a backwards glance, let alone a second thought. In that moment twenty-five years ago, as I openly shared my story—our story—with my family, I felt rejected all over again. With their refusal to accept the truth, the prolonged and violent child sexual abuse I suffered through was deemed to be my fault. And that is where the answer lies, as if my mother reacted as a normal mother, she would have to accept her own culpability. There was no way she could ever allow that to happen. So instead, she blamed me and I internalised it. It was that blame that kept me silent for decades. If it was my fault, then I must have been bad and deserved what I got. The cover-up continued.

It saddened me to realise that while time had moved forward, my mother's attitude had not. The mother who had abandoned me as a toddler, and again at eleven, had for a third time rejected me at thirty-two. Believing me was never an option for her; self-preservation was. I was constantly described as 'deluded', 'confused', 'brainwashed' or cast aside as 'the black sheep' of the family. Her reaction was calculated and clever—if it were all in my mind, no one could ever point the finger elsewhere. A strategic manipulation designed to take the focus off her, which worked to her advantage.

Three years after I revealed the truth, I was still not believed, and in fact was vilified, rejected and even held responsible for my mother's health issues. Despite my mother's alarming response to my disclosures, I was still processing my trauma and could not fully recognise that she was continuing to perpetrate her abuse of me even then. With her cunning and charm, she got away with it. Not only was she repeating history, but she also added to it and made it worse. Her decision to cast me aside was, I suspect, deeply unconscious, as she raised me the way she had been raised. Had my mother been loved and cherished as a child, perhaps I would have been as well. Nevertheless, nothing should or can excuse her wilful decision to hurt me, and let me be hurt, as a child and then an adult over and over again.

My mother would not leave it there, however. She took it to a level I hadn't expected, even from her. She had repeatedly warned me about discussing the events of my childhood with her, saying there would be consequences if I continued. One day, she followed through with her threat and suddenly cut me out of her life. In a four-page letter delivered to my letterbox, she informed me that I was not welcome to contact, phone or visit her ever again. Wow! After all the rejection and hurt I had endured over the years, this sliced open a fresh, deep wound. What made it even more difficult was that my relationship with my siblings had finally broken down as well. They took my mother's side, adamant that I should admit I was wrong. As I couldn't do that, our ties frayed until they snapped.

I could only take so much criticism and derision from my siblings before an unbreakable distance grew between us. I did a lot of grieving over the next few years, for my children and for myself as a rejected child. As a mother myself, I was aware of the impact on me. How could another mother do that to their child? And how could my mother do that to me?

Despite everything, over the next few months of no contact, I missed my mother dreadfully. It made me realise that that no matter how old or young I might be, I always held onto the hope that the one person who would stand by me and always be there for me was my mother. Even though deep down I knew she wouldn't, there was always a part of me that secretly hoped one day she might change. Her word had always been law growing up, which I still carried with me as an adult, but cutting me out of her life shook me up and made me start questioning her authority. It is only now, many years later, that I recognise how damaged she must have been to invest so much in the lies and cover-ups that kept the abuse secret. I was devastated, for myself and for my children who would miss out on having a relationship with their grandmother. I wanted my children to grow up surrounded by a loving family, to have what I was never provided.

I felt failed by anything 'family', so I determined that my children would never feel the pain of a dysfunctional and morally bankrupt mother themselves. My vow was to love them and be there for them so unconditionally that they would never have cause to question it.

I resolved to carry on. I had my children to raise and I was determined to give them a happy and loving home. What I hadn't allowed myself to recognise was the immense pain of losing my mother all over again. The traumatic and deeply painful impact of this felt like the death of a loved one. It got so bad that when I saw friends who had normal loving families, I would avoid discussing mine. I didn't want to share how hard my life was without one. I used to pretend everything was fine, but it became more difficult and more obvious as time went by that it wasn't.

Although it may sound bizarre, over twenty-five years I attempted several times to reintegrate myself back into my mother's life— occasionally with success, but never for more than a few years at a time. Her acceptance was always conditional. I was welcome in her life if I cut out the part of me that was honest about our early lives. Each time we eventually reconnected, I had to accept that, to do so, I could not stand in my own truth. As long as I compartmentalised and shut down who I really was and what really happened to me, I was welcomed back. In my desperation to build a family life I never had, I buried the truth, forgoing my own emotional needs to serve hers. Only then was I allowed to have a mother again.

I had always been the practical and supportive member of the family. I had been the one who would take round baking or meals for my mother and would regularly visit. I was the child living the closest to her geographically, and caregiving was inherent in my nature. For all my mother's flaws, I still saw the good in her. I saw a flicker of kindness, and I just wanted a mother in my life. Losing her in my thirties was so hard, but as I became more self-sufficient and realised I could live my life without her, she paradoxically started to show me more love to win me over and make me submit to her authority again.

Although looking back I never felt her love as a child and adolescent, as an adult I did. It has to be remembered that from my mid-teenage years I demanded nothing from her; it was entirely one sided, as I was firmly entrenched in the giving part of the relationship. I enjoyed helping her and giving her gifts, which worked for me as I was able to gain her acceptance. That felt safer than her neglect and abandonment. Although it was dysfunctional, I was still her youngest child and wanted her love and approval. I genuinely loved her, even though I knew she didn't deserve it, but I also knew she had never before experienced unconditional love in her life and I really wanted to show her it was possible.

Our relationship was never better than during those years and I was happy to have her in my life, so I kept suppressing the truth to keep this new bond alive. Compartmentalising came naturally to me—I had done it all my life. But as I grew and healed, I would eventually be required to face the truth of who I was, what I had experienced and what I needed to do to evolve more fully. I couldn't compartmentalise my life just to keep her secret. I had tried for years before realising I was just damaging myself further and it had to stop. It all came to a head when the final time she rejected me proved to be the most challenging of all.

In October 2013, my mother was turning eighty and she expressed that all she wanted for her birthday was for her children to reunite. I felt a bit awkward about this, simply because I had not had a relationship with them for so long. For her sake, I said I would, thinking I could handle it as I had done a lot of healing up to that point. I decided to have a positive outlook towards a possible reconciliation.

Well, that was my intent anyway, little did I know what was in store for me, as not only would it prove to be impossible, but the ultimate betrayal of all. On the day of my mother's birthday party, she had requested that all her children meet to see if we could find a way to patch up our differences and be a united family once again. I went in there believing that if I were just honest, it would be a good start. This proved to be a mistake, as although I had worked on myself over the years, it soon became clear that my siblings had not.

When I arrived, Shane exclaimed how good it was to see me again. He seemed genuine, and as we talked more, it became evident that he was the spokesperson for the group. It felt like a disappointing return to the patriarchal power dynamic in our family all those years ago, but I remembered that my siblings had all joined a fundamentalist Christian group and this was the way they operated. The men were still considered to be the most important people in their community, and as such they spoke on the group's behalf. It was awful to see my sisters relegated to supporting roles, without contributing anything meaningful.

As the conversation progressed and we discussed our families and our lives in more detail, I got the sense that all was not as it seemed. I decided to cut to the chase and emphasised that as Mum wanted us to reconnect, it would be important for us to get together over the next few days and discuss our situation in an honest and transparent manner.

Shane agreed, as long as we did 'not discuss anything to do with our childhoods'. If I could accept that, then he was happy to proceed. I was stunned. It had taken a lot for me to get to this point and make the effort I had in attending the birthday celebration for Mum's sake. None of this had been easy for me and yet as Shane spoke, a strong sense of déjà vu descended upon me. There was only one other person I had ever heard those words from, and that was my mother. As I delved further, he became even more emphatic that, 'Anything and everything else could be discussed, but *that*.' When I asked why, he said he didn't want to go into it.

Although I kept trying over the course of the afternoon, sadly it was not possible for us to reignite any familial relationships. Once again, I was made out to be the villain and it was all my fault. My desire to be open and honest with my siblings was deemed to be wrong. Although I wanted my mother's wish for a family reconciliation to be granted, I could not in all honesty pretend that we could all just pick up the pieces and patch them together after twenty years of silence without any honest discussion of why the family's relationship had broken down in the first place.

We were at an impasse.

While my mother's eightieth birthday went well overall (I certainly did what I could to make it work out for her), after a few days I went back up and saw her. I needed her to realise what had really happened and how the façade we had as siblings couldn't continue if she truly wanted us to be a family again. It just wasn't true, and it was hurting me to fake it to keep her and the others happy. I even asked her, very gently, if it was perhaps time for her to tell the truth. I encouraged her by saying that if she did that, she could right a terrible wrong and help to heal our family. She seemed to genuinely consider it for a moment, pausing, before saying, 'But if I do that, I make Shane out to be wrong and I can't do that to him.' I replied, 'Mum, he's had you standing beside him all of these years, perhaps you could stand by me, maybe it's my turn?' She looked uncomfortable in her moment of doubt, but as I didn't want to push her, the conversation ended there. I said goodbye to her and promised to be in touch.

The next day, I received an email from her sister, Margaret, telling me that I was not welcome to be part of the family if I carried on like this, and that unless I could be 'the Gloria everyone likes', I should stay away. She went on to say how disappointed in me she and her husband were and, furthermore, 'How dare I bully her sister like that.' I was stunned. Clearly, my mother had phoned Margaret and given her version of events. It broke my heart all over again. Once again, I had been deleted from the family. Once again, it was all my fault. Once again, I had no right of reply.

I never did respond to Margaret's email. Instead, I tried to contact my mother several times over the next week. She refused to answer me, which in itself was answer enough. Eventually, I got an email from her saying unless I apologised for the deep hurt I had caused her and promised to never mention my childhood again, I was not welcome in her life.

And there she was—the mother I had grown up with.

Just as before, I was again tossed aside so she could protect herself and her image at all costs. Supporting her youngest daughter was never her priority.

There was much heartache and sadness over these months and that particular Christmas was one of the hardest I had ever experienced. A lot of that had to do with my children, as not only had I been cut off from my mother, but they had, by association, been cut off from their grandmother. I had raised my children to be loving and respectful towards their grandmother and they had often helped her over the years. They had loved her unconditionally, had cooked for her, played music for her, included her in events in their lives and always been there for her. My mother was indifferent to the pain she caused them.

Once the shock had passed, I finally realised that I wasn't meant to have a family that loved me in this lifetime. It was a bitter pill to swallow and I struggled to get it down. In the end, I had no choice. I had to find a way to make peace with that. The pain of losing my mother and siblings, took me to a sad and lonely place and I felt bereft for months afterwards. It took me years to realise that as much as I had lost my family, they had also lost me and my children. They have missed out on so much over the years because of their inability to withstand my mother's rule and tell the truth.

To deal with the pain, I went within to find the inner strength I needed to keep living my life with integrity and kindness. It took every last ounce of my courage and tenacity not to sink into a dark place. I knew I had loving people around me who listened to me and supported me, but it was still my family I grieved for. One of the hardest things for me was not showing my children the enormous pain I felt. I wanted to protect them. They had also lost their family and I resolved not to make it any harder for them by showing them the absolute emptiness and misery I felt. This time though, suppressing my emotions to protect the wellbeing of others at the expense of my own felt like the right thing to do. Over time, we all eventually came to terms with it and accepted it for what it was.

A major challenge throughout my life has been to see myself as a loving, and lovable, person when my own mother has rejected me so many times. I have no doubt that if she could face me now, she would still reject me to protect herself. A mother's love, or in my case lack thereof, is powerful. I never stopped trying to have an honest relationship with her but the damage I suffered as a result of my attempts became too much. I couldn't continue knocking at a door she would never open, so in the end I chose truth and light over lies and darkness. Yet even though she was dysfunctional and cruel, she was still the only mother I had.

She never realised that she had so much more to gain than to lose had she allowed the truth to surface. Not only would she have been set free from her guilt and shame, but so would her children. She would have been able to help them heal and free them with the peace that only the truth can bring.

I fear my family's legacy has become bound by the secrets they keep. My wish for them is that one day they will find the courage to face them. My solace is knowing I can look at myself in the mirror and like what I see. I stand in my truth, I believe in who I am and I have become a light that can finally shine through.

POLICE INVESTIGATION

I was thirty-two years old when I decided to prosecute a case against my father for the childhood sexual, physical and emotional abuse he inflicted on me from birth until I was sixteen. This didn't suddenly happen, rather it came about at the suggestion of my family lawyer at the time. He sat down with me and asked me to tell him what had happened in my life. As I talked more about what I had experienced, he was suitably moved and asked for some documentation, which he subsequently took to a top criminal lawyer in New Zealand, who in turn went to the police.

The senior detective tasked with my case met me during the initial phase of the investigation, and right from the start he took the job seriously and showed me immense compassion which I am grateful for. The year was 1992 and his job was to work with a team to dig back through evidence of thirty years ago. He put seven detectives on my case who spent several months investigating via interviews with neighbours, friends, teachers, members of the local community, colleagues and church groups. They also needed to liaise with seedier underworld connections.

Their investigation was completed in a few short months and when they were ready they contacted me to report the findings. It wasn't good news.

The senior detective told me that although I would be a credible witness and though he would have no problem putting me on the stand, the findings from the investigation weren't quite so compelling. On a scale of one to ten, the findings placed the chances of my case succeeding at a six, whereas he would recommend a minimum of seven in order to proceed with a prosecution. He said I would be slammed with questions from the defence and crucified if my claims weren't backed up by harder evidence.

Although his team had investigated and spoken to many people, he said they still needed one more family member to step forward to substantiate my claims. With five out of my six family members refuting my claims, we were at an impasse. All he needed was for one more to cross over to my side and tell the truth, then he would have no hesitation in taking this to the High Court and initiating criminal proceedings against The Monster. Overall, he reported that sadly the benchmark to proceed was unable to be met, therefore they couldn't test my case in court. He was at pains to point out that this didn't mean there wasn't good evidence, just that there wasn't enough of it, and there was nothing more they could do until I could provide more proof.

He gave me the option of keeping the case open or closing it. After thinking long and hard, I came to accept that I had no idea where I would be able to find more evidence and so, with a heavy heart, I agreed to close the case. This was an exhausting and dispiriting time for me, but at least I knew I was always believed by police and had their ongoing support to pursue this matter further if I wished.

During the investigation, police officers spoke to my whole family including my parents. They were all interviewed at the Auckland Central Police Station by the detectives on the case. One of the things my mother proudly told me later was that on arriving at the police station, she offered to autograph copies of her books for the detectives interviewing her. Yes, you read that right. Her first response was to highlight her fame, rather than delve into the serious concerns raised about the perverted and evil crimes her daughter was subjected to. This did not go unnoticed by the team, and years later I was told they found that odd.

My decision to let my case be closed left me feeling disappointed, miserable and once again isolated. Not because of the work done by detectives on the case, but by the system. Once again, my parents had got away with the abuse they had inflicted on me over sixteen years. For some reason, justice was not meant to be served. Although it may be a closed case which was never taken to court, the fact remains that there was always a case to answer.

The police left me with something poignant. After interviewing my father, who vehemently denied the allegations, they told me they had never met a paedophile who ever willingly confessed and told the truth. Not once.

AFTERWORD

I have often been asked how I survived those sixteen years, and what stands out the most are my Angels. They were always with me with such love that I felt part of them and them me. My spirit soared from feeling their presence and that is what I am most grateful for, as without them I wouldn't be here. I didn't realise it was spiritual, I just thought I had magical friends with big white wings.

Among other factors, resilience was one of the most impactful. As a child, I didn't know what that meant, but looking back, I see just how much courage I needed to face every day of the hell I was born into. I needed to be resilient to withstand the repeated torture I suffered.

What surprised me in looking back was that, despite everything, I remained hopeful. I'm not sure why or where it came from, but I remember knowing that although I was suffering, there was something deep inside me that urged me to keep going.

Out of this pool of resources, the greatest of all was knowing that my spirit could not be broken.

If you would like to learn more about my recovery and how I navigated my way through those sixteen years, my next book in my *On Angels' Wings* series, *My Flightpath to Healing* shares how. It will detail the techniques I used and the solutions I developed to not just survive but thrive through my adult life. Follow my blog gloriamasters.com for free uplifting content and further information on release dates.

LATER

Because there were such dark times throughout my life, I used to feel victimised, isolated and sorry for myself. But as my circumstances weren't changing, I realised I needed to do something differently. If my life had taught me anything, it was that the only person I could rely on was myself, so I started with that. I went within and finally learned to open myself up to healing and light.

This didn't happen instantly. It would take many years before I learned that when I faced suffering, I could either accept and grow from it, or become a victim of it. As an adult, I initially chose the victim mentality, but all that did was keep me locked into the cycle of believing I was less than. Low self-esteem only served to attract more negativity into my being, which then manifested itself in all areas of my life. It didn't help me, there was no growth and it only led me through more suffering and helplessness.

Once I learned how to adapt to the suffering, I started to grow and ultimately see there was more to this world than I ever imagined. By identifying this, I started to heal and truly live. By reaching inward, not outward, I learned to discover who I really was. Because it worked for me, I saw it as the way forward to happiness and fulfilment.

NOW

As my formative years were filled with such trauma and suffering, it has been difficult to see how I could be a force for good in the world. I know now it is possible, which motivated me to write this book. What got me through, how my beliefs have changed, how I saw the world and what I could do to manage and survive. I have discovered that my life purpose is 'to help others by shining light onto darkness through love and humility'. It is a motto I live by. I don't know exactly know how to do that, but I do know it is my destiny and this book is a pathway to that. Whatever comes of it, however it manifests, that is the true purpose by which I am guided. I believe I am exactly where I should be, and I have no doubt that life is working for me not against me. Therefore, I am grateful. Grateful that I know this and that I am not resisting. It has taken a long time to work my way through the trauma and just trust.

To be able to share my story is a gift and I am humbled to offer hope and light to others. My wish in writing this book has always been that it reaches as many as possible who have also suffered from child sexual abuse, so freedom can be felt, and voices can be heard.

It is time to discover the real truth of who we are, by handing the shame back to the real owners: the perpetrators.

'All truth passes through three stages. First, it is ridiculed. Second, it is violently opposed. Third, it is accepted as being self-evident.'

Arthur Schopenhauer

Printed in Great Britain
by Amazon

22830743R00111